Curriculum Visions

Rich and poor in Tudor times

Teacher's Guide

More support material can be found
at the web site:

www.CurriculumVisions.com

You can also consult our web site:

www.AtlanticEurope.com

for material on a wide variety of topics
and our on-line catalogue.

Peter Riley and Brian Knapp

Atlantic Europe Publishing

First published in 2005 by Atlantic Europe Publishing Company Limited, Greys Court Farm, Greys Court, Henley-on-Thames, Oxfordshire RG9 4PG, United Kingdom.

ISBN 1 86214 429 X

Authors
Peter Riley, BSc, C Biol, MI Biol, PGCE
Brian Knapp, BSc, PhD

Art Director
Duncan McCrae, BSc

Senior Designer
Adele Humphries, BA, PGCE

Editor
Gillian Gatehouse

Illustrations
David Woodroffe

Designed and produced by
EARTHSCAPE EDITIONS

Printed in China by
WKT Company Ltd.

Acknowledgements
Atlantic Europe Publishing would like to thank the teachers and pupils who trialled the activities for this book on their 'Tudor day'.

Contents

> Includes tried and tested ideas for planning your own Tudor day on pages 10–15.

Section 1: 'Rich and poor in Tudor times' resources

The resources

Welcome to *Curriculum Visions Rich and poor in Tudor times*. The resources available are in four parts:

❶ *Rich and poor in Tudor times*, a 48-page, full-colour student paperback book that provides comprehensive coverage of the lives of the rich and poor in Tudor times.

❷ A PosterCard Portfolio, designed to show the main features of life in Tudor times. This portfolio also allows you to have large pictures that you can make the basis of your own worksheets.

❸ This *Teacher's Guide*. It contains practical guidance and photocopiable worksheets featuring a range of activities which reinforce the content of the student book and help the children appreciate a little of what life was like in Tudor times and how historians and archaeologists work to build up a picture of the past.

❹ The web site. It contains page-by-page support for *Rich and poor in Tudor times* and can be used, for example, to provide material for projects and for children working from home who have an Internet connection.

▼ *Rich and poor in Tudor times* **student book and PosterCard Portfolio.**

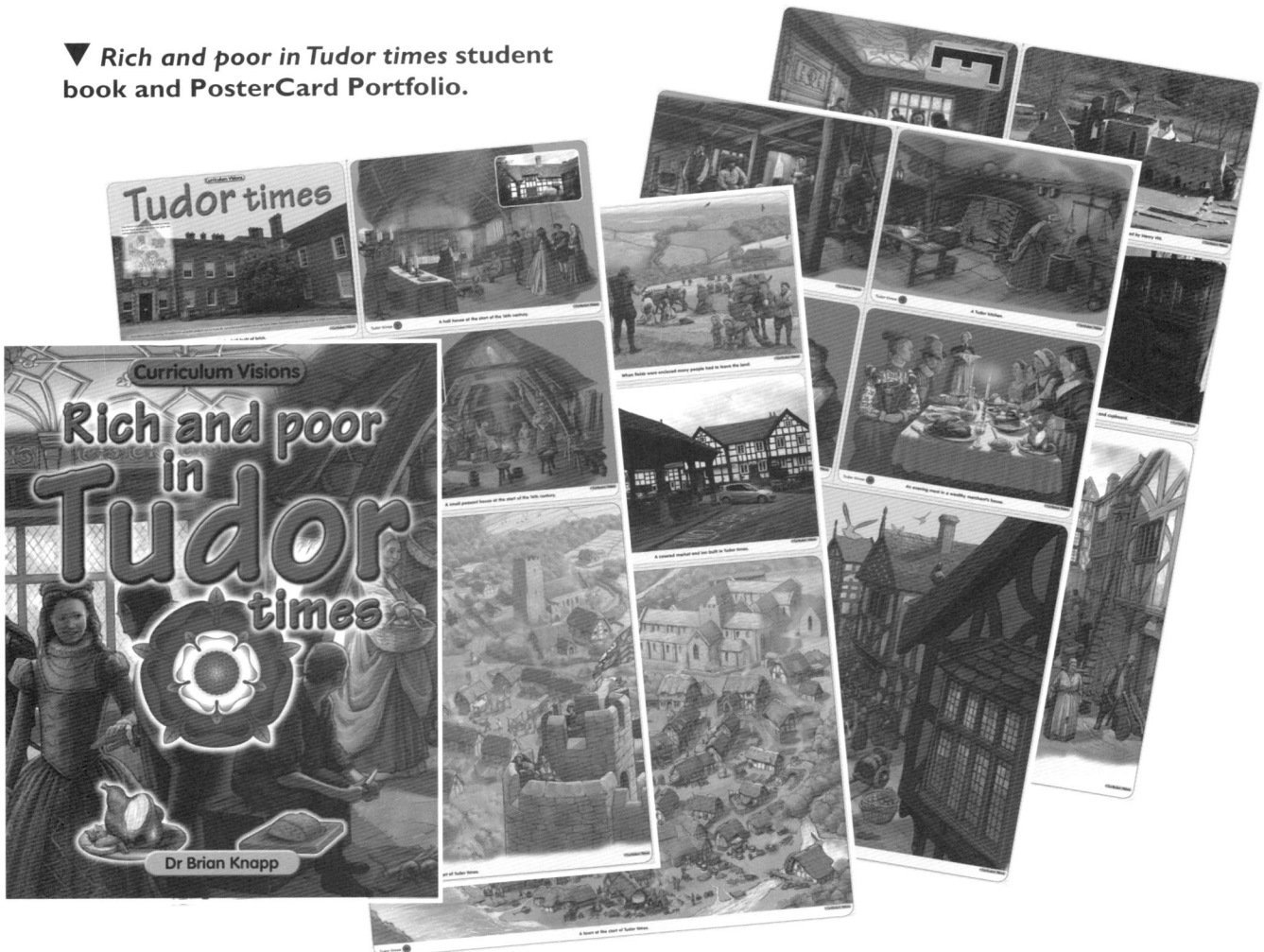

4

Please note that the detail shown on these screens may change as new materials are added regularly.

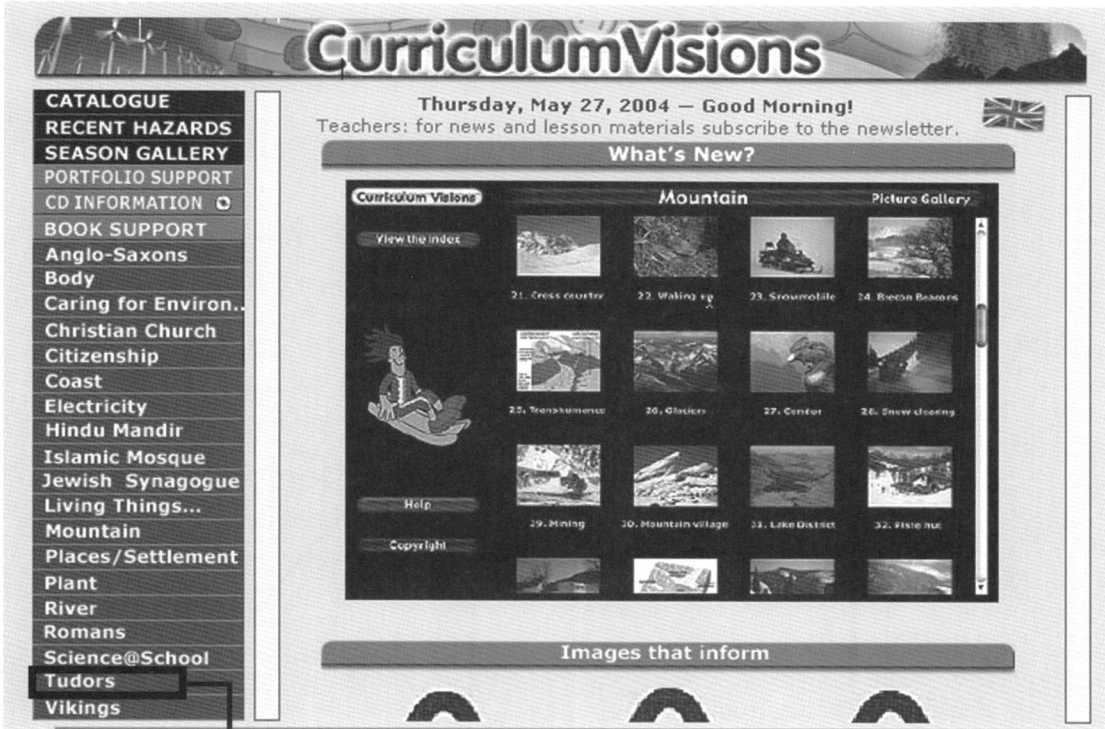

▲▼ The *Curriculum Visions.com* web site home screen and its link to *Rich and poor in Tudor times*.

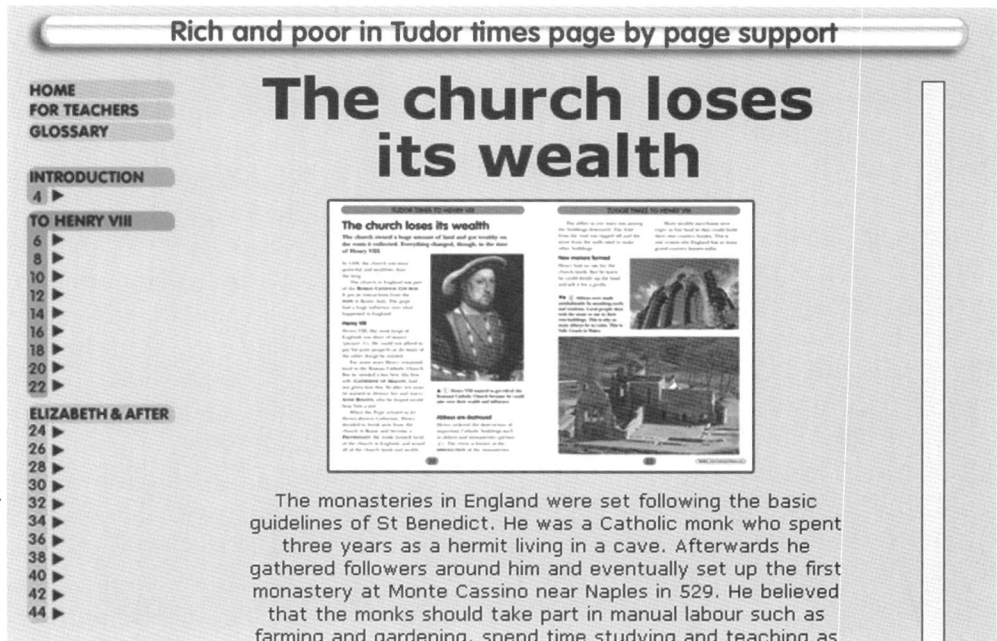

The monasteries in England were set following the basic guidelines of St Benedict. He was a Catholic monk who spent three years as a hermit living in a cave. Afterwards he gathered followers around him and eventually set up the first monastery at Monte Cassino near Naples in 529. He believed that the monks should take part in manual labour such as farming and gardening, spend time studying and teaching as

Matching the curriculum

These resources of books, PosterCard Portfolio and web site aim to ensure that students:

- Find out about people and important events and developments from recent and more distant times.
- Make links across different periods of history.
- Learn about different aspects of local, British and world history.
- Have the chance to discuss why things happened or changed, and the results.
- Can carry out historical enquiries using a variety of sources of information, and look at how and why the past is interpreted in different ways.
- Can use their understanding of chronology and historical terms when talking or writing about the past.
- Learn about the experiences of people in the past, and why they acted as they did.
- Develop respect for and tolerance of other people and cultures.
- See how people in the past have changed the society in which they lived.
- Develop respect for evidence, and the ability to be critical of the evidence.
- Develop an understanding of right and wrong and the ability to handle moral dilemmas.
- Understand, and adjust for some popular myths and stereotypes.

Furthermore, because history provides so many opportunities for improving communication skills, the resources aim to provide a body of material that can be used to reinforce English studies and which could, for example, be used in a literacy hour.

Last, and by no means least, these history resources can be linked to many other subjects, particularly settlement and water (geography) through the *Curriculum Visions Places Pack* and *Water Pack*, and through the use of science where appropriate.

Curriculum Visions products are renowned as a successful way to help teachers to get children of all abilities, ages and ethnic backgrounds to develop confidence in themselves, and to make the most of their abilities through the wide range of materials, the different levels of reading skills represented on each page,

and through the wide range of tasks in the photocopiable worksheets.

It should be noted that this material has been designed to be accessible by those teaching Tudors in years 3/4 or 5/6 (SP4/5 or 6/7). This can be done with the help of the teacher by selective use of the worksheet material and by using the information in the student book to go in to the appropriate level of depth.

Teaching with the pack

The material has been written and presented to cover a range of curricular requirements. The components of the pack provide you with the flexibility to teach the curriculum in whatever way you wish.

1. Using the student book

Rich and poor in Tudor times is a 48-page full colour paperback student book arranged systematically to cover basic historical principles.

By working through the book and using the worksheets in this *Teacher's Guide*, it is easy to cover the requirements of the curriculum.

Rich and poor in Tudor times provides a foundation for understanding the Rich and poor in Tudor times by making comparisons in dress, food and housing. The development of villages and towns at the beginning of Tudor times is considered along with important events such as the Armada, the Plague and the attempt to settle in the New World.

An explanation of the teaching points of each spread is given in this *Teacher's Guide*, just before the worksheets covering each spread.

Each double-page spread in *Rich and poor in Tudor times* forms the basis for a teaching unit. The book is designed to be used sequentially, although each spread is self-contained and can be used in isolation if you wish. This makes the material exceptionally flexible for your needs.

The spread at the front of *Rich and poor in Tudor times* (pages 4 to 5) features the

Tudor monarchs, an explanation of why many Tudors were so poor and a timeline of important events. It can be used to set the scene for studying Tudor life in the rest of the book.

2. Using the PosterCard Portfolio

You may wish to start the topic by displaying the PosterCard Portfolio, and then leaving the sheets on display throughout the time the course is being taught. You can use the cards in a whole-class presentation and students can also use them for reference purposes. Furthermore, you can cut them up and use them for your own worksheets.

3. Using the Teacher's Guide

This *Teacher's Guide* brings together all of the resources for *Rich and poor in Tudor times*, and gives an overview of each resource. It also contains a very extensive selection of worksheets.

Please note that there may be several worksheets matching a spread in *Rich and poor in Tudor times*.

This will allow some students to develop the subject more extensively, and exercise skill in historical or archaeological technique or reinforce a skill in another subject, such as English or science, to provide a cross-curricular dimension to their work. Alternatively one worksheet may be used for years 3 to 4 and the other for years 5 to 6.

4. Using the web site in school or at home

Every topic in *Rich and poor in Tudor times* is matched by a page on our dedicated web site.

To get to this page on the web site, open your browser and type:

www.curriculumvisions.com

into the 'Location' or 'Address' bar near the top of the browser window. When you get the home screen, click on 'Tudors' in the book list.

The purpose of the page by page support on the web site is:

- To provide extra information on each topic for the more able students.
- To provide extra case studies.
- To promote ICT skills.
- To show students that information about the subject can be presented in a variety of media.
- To allow students to find an informative web site on curriculum-related material when they are surfing the Internet at home.

5. Links

Rich and poor in Tudor times can be linked to other books in the *Curriculum Visions* series, particularly *Places*.

Section 2: Background and photocopiable worksheets

Introduction

Each spread of the student book is supported by background information and photocopiable worksheets in this *Teacher's Guide*. They have been designed to be a fast and efficient way of working through the study of 'Rich and poor in Tudor times'.

Variety and selection

Each photocopiable worksheet is supported by information on its facing page which includes a resources list (where appropriate), suggestions on how the worksheet may be used and outcomes that may be achieved. There are probably more worksheets than you would use with any particular class, so it is important to have a look through them all, and select which ones you wish to use to support your approach to the study of Tudor times.

Linking background and worksheet to the student book

Each section of background information and each worksheet has been given a unique number which is in a circle at the top of the page. This is related to the number of the spread in the book. For example, pages 4 and 5 are spread ❶ and pages 6 and 7 are spread ❷. If there is more than one worksheet per student book spread, then they are labelled A, B, and so on. At the head of each worksheet are the relevant pages of *Rich and poor in Tudor times* for easy reference for students. They may find it useful to look back in the student book to help them with the activity on the worksheet. If the worksheet is testing understanding or evaluation of the information based on the spread, it will be essential for the students to use the student book with the worksheet. Some of the worksheets provide instructions for practical activities which support the topic covered in the spread.

A closer look at the worksheets
Cross-curricular work

The worksheets provide a wide range of activities for the students. The aim of the worksheets is to help the students appreciate what it was like to live in Tudor times.

Some of the worksheets look at how we gather evidence using simple archaeological investigations and how the results of these investigations can be interpreted. Many students enjoy popular television programmes about archaeology.

The purpose of the archaeology worksheets is to build on this interest and show in the context of 'Rich and poor in Tudor times' how some archaeological techniques help us make discoveries about the past.

Following many discoveries, experiments are made to test ideas. These are also featured on some of the worksheets to allow you to do some cross-curricular work with science, technology and English. Indeed, in a packed curriculum, it is often difficult to find time to explore some topics like 'Rich and poor in Tudor times', in the way you wish. We hope by providing a variety of worksheets, which you can also use for addressing literacy, science and geography, that you can make studying 'Rich and poor in Tudor times' a rich experience for your students.

Spanish Armada map

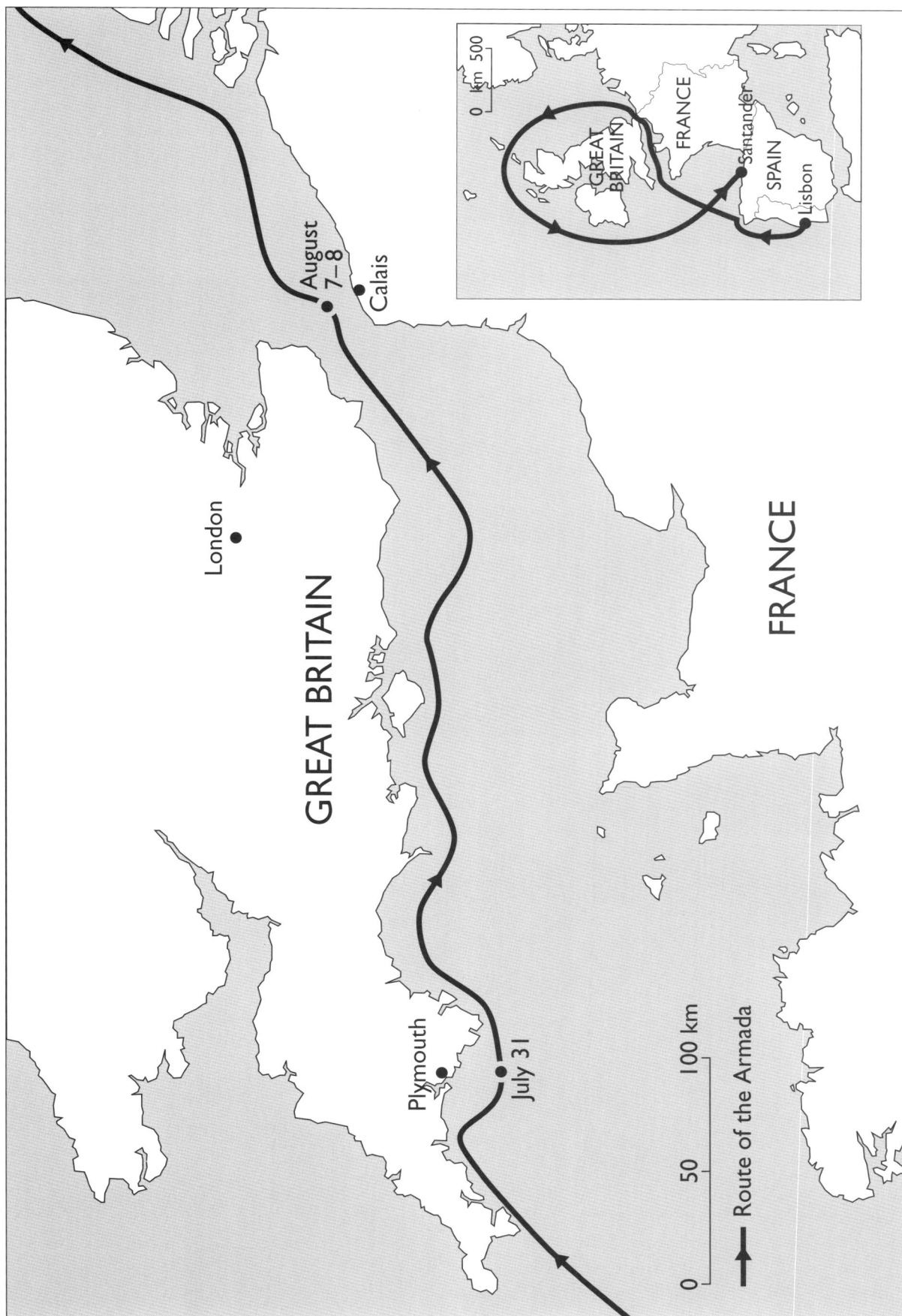

Route of the Armada

0   50   100 km

GREAT BRITAIN

London

Calais

August 7–8

Plymouth

July 31

FRANCE

0 km 500

FRANCE

GREAT BRITAIN

SPAIN

Santander

Lisbon

Organising a Tudor day

A Tudor day at school can be an enjoyable, memorable and educational experience for the students (and teachers and support staff!). It needs plenty of planning to run smoothly so if you are considering having a Tudor Day as part of your coverage of teaching 'Rich and poor in Tudor times' we hope that these notes and pictures will help you have a successful day.

Support from home

You will need support from home for the making of costumes and the making of a Tudor meal so a pleasant letter to homes explaining your plans will help start the project moving. You may find that some parents and carers are very enthusiastic and may volunteer ideas and resources.

▲▼ Looking forward to the day's activities.

▶ Rich Tudors...

▲ Dressing up for the day.

▶ Poor Tudors...

Costumes

Tudor costumes ranged from rags to royal clothes. You may like to show the students a range of clothes as illustrated in the student book and let them work with their parents or carers on making a suitable costume. You will find that on the day the students will present a range of costumes from simple citizen to Henry VIII or Elizabeth I. It would be useful to have two or three basic costumes made by you or the school staff for students who for any reason do not have a costume on the day. One way to make sure that everyone feels like a rich Tudor is to make a simple ruff as shown in activity **2B** page 26 (and pictured on page 13).

You will also need to consider when the costumes are worn. Do you want them to wear the costumes all day and go out at breaks and lunch-times in them? Do you want them to be worn after morning break, through lunch-time to afternoon break or do you just want them to be worn in the afternoon?

► Bringing in a 'Tudor' lunch (link to science 'food, teeth and eating').

Food

The students could make up a Tudor lunchbox and bring it to school. A selection of Tudor food is given in activity **16B** page 108. You may like to use this as a basis for planning meals.

Rich Tudors loved marzipan, and activity **16A** page 106 gives a recipe on how to make it. You may like the students to make marzipan at home and bring it with them for the Tudor meal.

Rich Tudors drank wine; the students could drink fruit juice.

▼ Talking about Tudor writing.

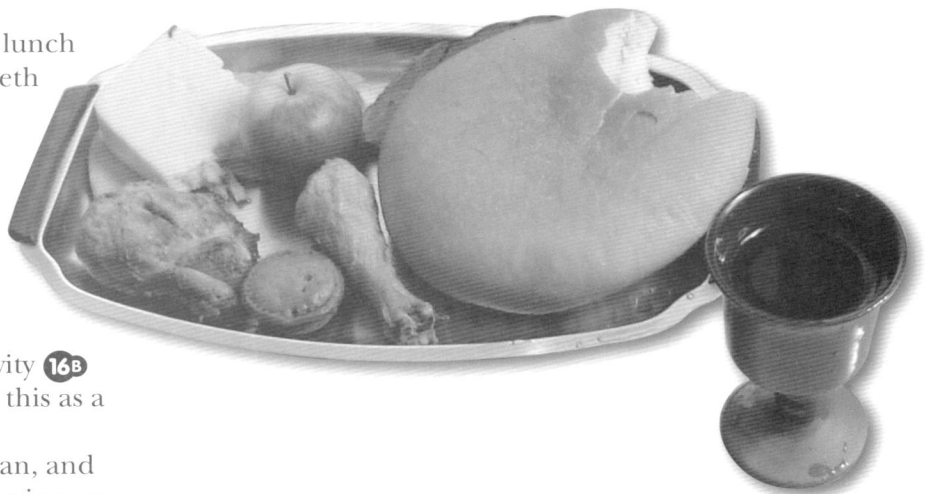

Setting the scene

A little while before the Tudor day you may like to try two scene setting activities. Activity **2C** page 28 'Make your own coat of arms', allows the students to make coats of arms which can be hung around the classroom to make it appear like a hall in a Tudor mansion. Activity **8** page 64 'Make a pomander' needs to be done two weeks before the Tudor day and the pomanders set up in the classroom the night before to give off an authentic Tudor smell.

Activities on the day

First session

You could begin by writing the date on the blackboard in Tudor style as shown in activity **6C** page 54 'Spell as you like'.

The role play featured in activity **1A** page 18 'Going back in time' may help the students to appreciate how long ago the Tudors lived.

Groups of students may be engaged in the following activities and at the end they can pool their work to show a little of what life was like in a Tudor school:

Make a horn book (activity **19A** page 120).
Make a pen (activity **19C** page 124).
Black lettering (activity **19B** page 122).
Spell as you like (activity **6C** page 54).
Alternatively the students could try Beggars and thieves (activity **6A** page 50).
Can you understand these rogues? (activity **7** page 60).

▲▶ Making ruffs.

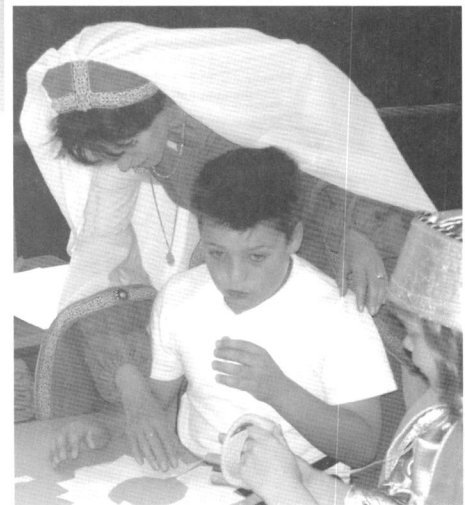

▲▶ Making a horn book.

◀ Making wattle and daub.

Second session

Money (activity **6B** page 52).
What did he leave behind? (activity **15** page 102).
Make a board game called Merelles (activity **14** page 98).

The Tudor lunch

(See notes on food above.)

Afternoon sessions

The students could break into groups and each group work on one of these activities:

(You may like to enlist the help of support staff and school volunteer helpers to supervise the activities and give general help to the groups of students.)

Wattle and daub (activity **5** page 46).
Make a leaded window (activity **9A** page 68).
Make a house (activity **13B** page 92).
Dating wood with tree rings (activity **13C** page 94).
Make a plague mask (activity **18** page 116).

The day could end with a dance:
Can you dance (activity **9B** page 70).

▼▶ Tudor dancing.

Chapter 1: Introduction

Spread ① (pages 4–5)

Tudor times

The purpose of this spread

The book starts with a simple timeline. As historical facts can easily become confusing, the purpose of this spread is to produce a simple perspective so that students know where they are going.

Background

The background of the whole book is based on the time of the Tudors. It was an extraordinary time in the history of England of less than a century and a half. It saw England blossom from being the poor man of Europe and far behind many other countries, to being one of the most powerful countries of Europe.

It also saw profound changes in the way people lived, in no small part due to the break with Rome. At a stroke, the head of the church became the king, the church became far less powerful, enormous wealth changed hands from those of the church to those of the king, and was realised as the king sold off church lands to the newly enriched middle class.

During the reign of the Tudors, far more people were able to live in comfort in the countryside than ever before. City merchants were able to buy a piece of land that had once belonged to the church. Here they could build their baronial halls and become squires and pillars of the country society.

Yeomen and others were also better off. They were able to rebuild or modify their homes and use materials that have survived through to the present day – the first time that this had been true for ordinary dwellings. The era of the 'black and white housing' typifies the change.

But at the same time, not everything was well with the country. The very poor became poorer. There was a drift of people from the countryside to the towns and cities. Whereas people had once relied on the church for help when they were poor, now they had to rely on the parish. And the parish was much more concerned not to support any from outside than the church had been.

It was also a time when England began to look overseas, to begin the foundations of her eventual empire and to take on the role of global explorer. The astounding round the world voyages took place in Tudor times, as did the first faltering steps at setting up a colony in the New World. Some of these were successful, some were less so. Some were disasters. But on the whole events moved forward thanks to long periods of firm government.

But many of these ideas are very sophisticated for students making their first foray into the Tudor world. To help them with this, the book looks at the changes that took place between about 1500 and 1600. It looks at fashions and houses, at villages and towns and also glimpses at the wider world of the Armada, exploration and settlement. In the timeline on pages 4 and 5 it also sets out the political events that took place. The traumatic political events that occurred repeatedly through this period are not covered here, for that would need a separate book.

What students should be able to do is to try to find evidence of these times near to them and to try to imagine what life must have been like.

Based on **pages 4 and 5** of Rich and poor in Tudor times

Going back in time

Cut out the information about each year and arrange the years in order starting with the most recent at the top.

1750 George II (1727–1760). In 1750 Joseph Fry invented the chocolate bar. The Seven Years War began in 1756 when England and France fought over who should rule North America and India.

2000 Elizabeth II (1953–   ). In 2003 Britain was involved in the war in Iraq. In 1998 Dolly the sheep was the first large animal to be cloned. DVDs began to replace videos in 1998.

1850 Victoria (1837–1901). In 1851 the Great Exhibition took place at Crystal Palace to show Britain's huge industrial achievements. Britain took part in the Crimean War in 1853.

1650 England was ruled by Parliament. In 1653 Oliver Cromwell ruled England as Lord Protector of the Commonwealth until his death in 1658. In 1650 the first coffee house was opened in London.

1900 Victoria (1837–1901). Britain was taking part in the second Boer War (1899–1902) in Africa. In 1901 gramophone records were available in the shops.

1800 George III (1760–1820). The Napoleonic wars began in 1802, and in 1805 The Battle of Trafalgar took place when Admiral Nelson defeated Napolean's forces and prevented England being invaded. Richard Trevithick invented the steam locomotive in 1801.

1950 George VI (1936–1952). The Second World War had ended five years previously in 1945. The hovercraft was invented in 1953.

1600 Elizabeth I (1533–1603). In 1600 newspapers were first published in England and William Shakespeare's Hamlet was first performed. In 1608 the telescope was invented in Holland. This led to Galileo using one to investigate space and make many discoveries.

1700 William III (1694–1702) Isaac Newton wrote about how he used a prism to investigate the colours in light.

Going back in time

Age range
- Years 3/4 (SP4/5).
- Years 5/6 (SP6/7).

Resources
Scissors, blank sheet of paper, sticky tape.
Optional for role play – Large (baby sized) doll, strips of cloth to make swaddling bands, present day baby's clothing.

Using the worksheet
The purpose of the worksheet is to let the children appreciate how far back in time the Tudors lived. You may use it simply as a timeline making exercise or you can take it further with the role play activity. The fifty year time gaps have been chosen to represent the life span of a person. As war and violence were a part of Tudor times in this timeline wars are also mentioned if they come close to the date in question. Also everyday items, instances of scientific importance or technological achievements are mentioned to provide a wider view. You may wish to add to these (see below) or bring the item on 2000 right up to date.

Younger students
The students can cut out the statements about each year and stick them on a sheet in the correct order. They could use other sources to find out about the other monarchs who are missing from the timeline. You may also like them to take part in a version of the role play activity.

Outcomes
The students can:
- Construct a timeline.
- Use secondary sources for research.

Older students
The students can cut out the statements about each year and stick them on the sheet in the correct order. They can then use other sources to find out about each of the monarchs mentioned. They should find out when they were born and work out their ages when they came to the throne. As things were clearly different in 1650, they may like

to find out more and report to the rest of the class. Alternatively they could create timelines about the discovery of everyday things as a way of finding out what was not available to the Tudors.

Outcomes
The students can:
- Construct a timeline.
- Use secondary sources for research.
- Perform calculations on dates.

Role play activity
People sometimes reflect on what the world was like when they were born. This idea can be developed into a role play activity. Tudor babies were wrapped tightly in swaddling bands. This was believed to help them grow well. You could wrap a baby-sized doll in bands of cloth a couple of centimetres wide and over thirty centimetres long. The doll is then dressed in present day baby clothing.

Tell the class that the fifty year period in the timeline represents a life time so we can get some idea of how far back the Tudors were by performing this activity. The baby is placed in a cot by someone representing today. The person then talks to the baby and using the information in the item on the timeline tells the baby about the world it has been born into. The person steps aside and a second person, this time from 1950, steps up to the baby and tells it about the world it has been born into. This person then lines up next to the first person. Other people follow and the line is made with the person representing the most recent time furthest from the baby. When the Tudor person has said their piece, they pick up the baby and remove its modern day clothes to show the class what babies wore in Tudor times. If you have the resources you may like the students to dress up in costumes from the time they represent.

A Tudor timeline

Mary I (1516–1558) She became queen in 1553. Mary tried to turn the country from a Protestant country back into a Catholic country.

Henry VIII (1491–1547). Henry became king in 1509. He changed England from a Catholic country into a Protestant one and made himself head of the Church of England. He closed the monasteries and used their wealth for himself. He made the English Navy the most powerful in Europe. Henry had three children – Edward, Mary and Elizabeth.

Henry VII (1457–1509). Henry was the Earl of Richmond who defeated Richard III at the Battle of Bosworth Field. This was the final battle in the Wars of the Roses. In 1485 he became king and married Elizabeth of York. Like almost everyone in Europe, Henry was a Catholic. He had a son called Henry.

Elizabeth I (1533–1603). Elizabeth became queen in 1558. She turned the country back into a mainly Protestant country. Her right to the throne was challenged by Mary Queen of Scots. Mary was imprisoned but was involved in a plot to have Elizabeth killed and was eventually executed.

Edward VI (1537–1553). Edward became king in 1547 but was too young to rule. The country was governed first by the Duke of Somerset and then by the Earl of Warwick and the Duke of Northumberland. They continued to keep England a Protestant country.

1. Cut out the details about each monarch and make them into a timeline based on the time when they were crowned. Start with the most recent monarch.

2. How old was each monarch when they came to rule?

   Henry VII .... Henry VIII .... Edward VI .... Mary I .... Elizabeth I ....

3. The Tudor period began when the first monarch was crowned and the last monarch died. How long was the Tudor period? ✎ ....

4. If you could have lived throughout the Tudor times and followed the wishes of the monarch how many times would you have changed religion? ✎ ....

5. (i) Arrange the three children of Henry VIII in order of when they were born, starting with the first to be born.

   ✎ .... ✎ .... ✎ ....

   (ii) Does this timeline match the order in which they reigned? Explain your answer.

   ✎ ....

A Tudor timeline

Age range
- Years 3/4 (SP4/5).
- Years 5/6 (SP6/7).

Resources
Scissors, sticky tape, a piece of white paper.

Using the worksheet
Although the main thrust of the topic is 'Rich and poor in Tudor times', you may feel that the students need a little background. This activity helps them to understand a little of the monarchy at the time. If you have done the previous activity, you may like to introduce this one by reminding the students that they had reached back to Elizabeth I, the last Tudor monarch. This activity introduces them briefly to the others.

Younger students
Let the students read through the items on the monarchs and cut them out. Remind them that they must be arranged by looking at the date when the monarch came to power and not when the monarch was born. When all the questions have been answered the students could compare the ages at which the monarchs came to rule and the lengths of their reigns.

Outcomes
The students can:
- Construct a timeline.
- Perform calculations using the dates.
- Suggest a reason for an anomaly in the timeline.

Older students
Let the students work through the questions. When they have finished, they could use other sources to find out about the Wars of the Roses, the Catholic Church, Protestants, how Mary Queen of Scots believed she had a right to the throne of England.

Outcomes
The students can:
- Construct a timeline.
- Perform calculations using dates.
- Use sources to carry out further research.

Answers
1. Henry VII, Henry VIII, Edward VI, Mary I, Elizabeth I.
2. Mary I 37, Henry VIII 18, Henry VII 28, Elizabeth I 25, Edward VI 10.
3. 118 years.
4. Three times.
5. (i) Mary, Elizabeth, Edward.
   (ii) No, Edward reigned first although he was the youngest. He reigned first because he was the son.

Chapter 2: Tudor times to Henry VIII

Spread ❷ (pages 6–7)

A big gap between rich and poor

The purpose of the spread

One of the ways in which we remember Tudor times is through images of the monarchs, and in particular Henry VIII and Elizabeth I.

Plays and other reconstructions are also common, so the dress of the day may not be too uncommon.

But the dress we usually see belongs, of course, to a tiny elite. It is not relevant to the majority of people.

One of the most interesting things to look at is the way that people dressed at court. They were just as fashion conscious as we are today. Styles changed repeatedly as people sought to be 'with it'.

Students can see this through using a wide variety of pictures from the time, for example, if they know the exact date of the picture.

There is considerable scope to try to look in detail at the clothing worn at court and to dress up and act out certain parts.

The idea of looking waspish, for example, was an important one for many women who were involved in keeping up with fashion. It allows us to consider what is fashion through the ages.

It might also be worth exploring the Tudor idea of public and personal hygiene. Many students would not dream that it was uncommon to wash and that Elizabeth, for example, was considered to be odd because she washed at least a few times a year.

Students might consider what happened when you did not wash. How did you cope with the body odour? Did this matter in a world where odours would be quite commonplace in the streets and elsewhere? Do we have an over anxiety with hygiene today, or was the lack of hygiene in Tudor times a contribution to disease?

It took a fashionable lady many hours to get dressed as there were many items to an outfit. The first to be put on was a chemise-smock (a loose fitting dress which hung from the shoulders). Over this was worn a petticoat. Next a lacy bodice (a sleeveless garment) was put on. This was followed by a skirt which may be supported by hoops and pad to make it stick out. A second bodice and skirt were worn on top of the other clothes. The bodice would have sleeves and perhaps a ruff. Finally a gown or cloak was worn. Knitted stockings were worn. Originally they were made of wool but later rich women wore silk as it became available through trade with the east. Slippers and shoes were worn.

Rich men also wore several layers of clothing. The most valuable part of a gentleman's wardrobe was his cloak which may have cost several hundred pound in Elizabethan times and may be the equivalent of someone driving a very expensive car today. The point about Raleigh spreading his cloak over a puddle so the Queen could pass by was that he was prepared to sacrifice a great deal for his monarch.

Married women and men wore hats. They were made of velvet, taffeta, felt, silk, ermine and beaver and were highly decorated. Unmarried women did not wear hats. It was polite for men to wear their hats indoors. If they were at court in Elizabethan times they had to take them off as the Queen entered or left the room.

Choose your Tudor costume

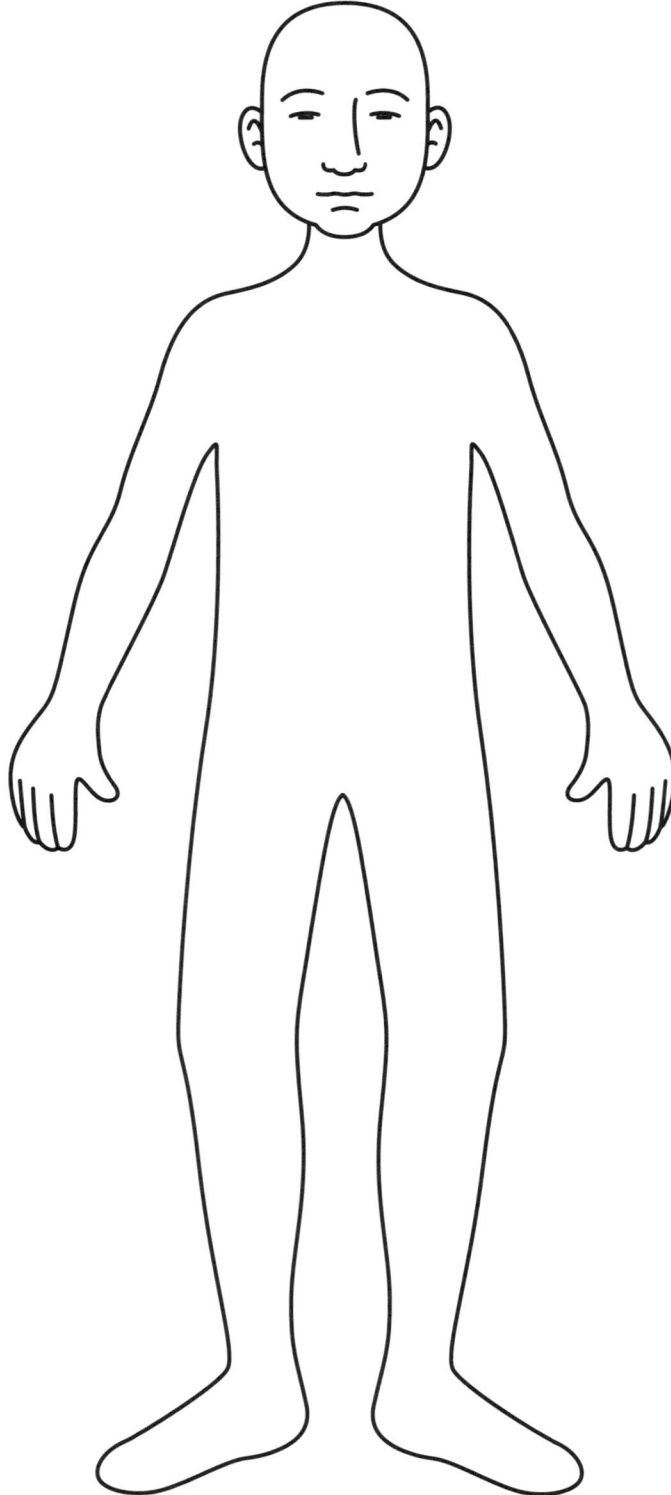

Choose your Tudor costume

Age range
- Years 3/4 (SP4/5).
- Years 5/6 (SP6/7).

Resources
Secondary sources about clothes in Tudor times. They should feature the clothes of both the rich and the poor.

Using the worksheet
You may like to use this as a lead into having a Tudor day when as many students as possible can dress up in a Tudor costume. The clothes of the poor are much easier to make than the clothes of the rich so you may use this activity to look at the clothes of the rich, and on the Tudor day the students can be dressed in the clothes of the poor. If there are colleagues or parents who are skilled in costume making, some clothes of the rich may be made to provide balance. The worksheet could also be used to plan the costume to be made.

Younger students
Let the students look through secondary sources and select costumes to draw and colour in on the worksheet. You could give them two worksheets – one for drawing the clothes of the poor and one for drawing clothes of the rich.

Outcomes
The students know that rich people:
- Dressed differently to poor people.
- Wore more clothes than poor people.
- Wore clothes made of finer materials than poor people.

Older students
As the Tudor period lasted over a century you could ask the students if the clothes worn by the people changed over that time. They should have access to sources which cover the whole period and conclude that fashions did indeed change for the rich but not much for the poor. They may use two worksheets – one to show a costume of a rich male or female from the beginning of the Tudor period and one from the end of the period.

Outcomes
The students can:
- Know that fashions changed in Tudor times.
- Recognise fashions from the early Tudor times.
- Recognise fashions from later Tudor times.

Make a ruff

1. Take two copies of this half ruff. Cut them out and turn one round so that they can be placed together to make a full ruff.

2. Take a piece of A4 paper and cut a strip from it about 2 cm wide and the full length of the sheet.

3. Wrap the strip around your neck. If you need more paper to reach right round your neck cut another strip and stick it to the first.

4. Mark the length of the strip that fits comfortably round you neck.

5. Make the strip into a circle and rest it in the centre of the ruff. Draw round the circle of paper then cut out a hemisphere from each ruff.

6. Use sticky paper to join one part of the ruff together. Put the ruff around your neck and use a white paperclip to join the other part.

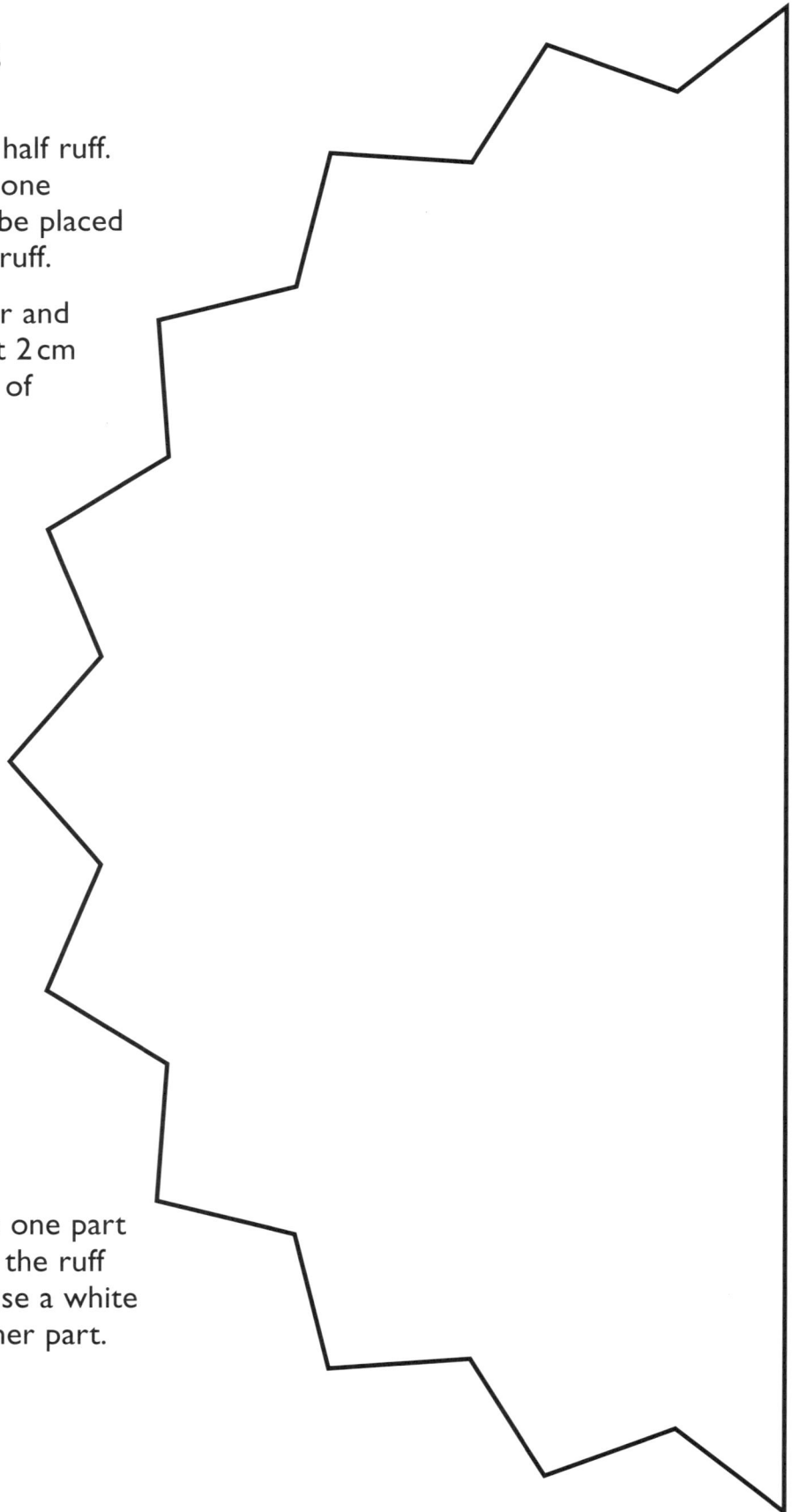

Make a ruff

Age range

- Years 3/4 (SP4/5).
- Years 5/6 (SP6/7).

Resources

Two photocopies of the worksheet, scissors, sticky paper, white paperclip, pencil. For older students white cards, doilies.

Using the worksheet

The ruff is a very distinctive item of Tudor clothing but it was not worn by poor people. The students can make a very simple one quite quickly in this activity and perhaps wear it for the rest of the lesson.

Younger students

Show the students how the two halves of the ruff are cut out and set up together on a table top. The students may need help in making a strip to fasten round their neck. The strip of card is really a collar so they need a little extra space for comfort. The collar is then placed in the centre of the ruff and the students lightly sketch in its position. They then discard the collar and cut around the line they have drawn in. Some students may need help joining two parts of the ruff with a paperclip.

Outcomes

The students:
- Know that the ruff was widely worn in Tudor times.
- Can make a model of a simple ruff and wear it.

Older students

When the older students have made their ruff, they could look at a range of ruffs in secondary sources. They could then design and make a more complex ruff perhaps using card and lacy paper doilies.

Outcomes

The students can:
- Make a model of a simple ruff and wear it.
- Use secondary sources to research the range of ruffs in the Tudor period.
- Design and make their own ruffs.

Make your own coat of arms

Make your own coat of arms

Age range
- Years 3/4 (SP4/5).
- Years 5/6 (SP6/7).

Resources
A photocopy of the sheet. Secondary sources on heraldry.

Using the worksheet
You may wish to use this sheet as an introduction to the rich in Tudor times. You could begin by talking about life before Tudor times, when most men in the upper classes of society expected to have to fight in at least one battle in their lives. Success in battle lead to a knighthood and the right to have a coat of arms. This comprised a shield (the surface is called the field (see below), a crest and two supporters of the shield. When a knight went into battle, he had the crest on his helmet and the markings of the field on his shield. This was so he could be identified, as his face was hidden under the visor of his suit of armour. In more peaceful times, the family of the knight could display his coat of arms on their property, such as over a door or fireplace. The coat of arms could be passed down through the generations of a family so coats of alms developed in the twelfth and thirteen centuries were still used by families in Tudor times as they are by some families today.

Younger students
Let the students make a design of their own shield and select a crest and supporters on the sides of the shield from secondary sources. Each student could make a large copy of the shield on card and display it on the wall of the classroom with the shields of others in readiness for a Tudor day.

Outcomes
The students know:
- The components of a coat of arms.
- How a family came to have a coat of arms.

Older students
The students could also make their own shields but also learn a little of the vocabulary of heraldry. If they made a visit to a Tudor mansion, where coats of arms are on display, they could use the vocabulary to describe what they see.

The surface of the shield is called the field. The upper part is the chief. If you were wearing the shield, the right hand side is called the dexter and the left is called the sinister.

The colours have their own names too: red (gules), blue (azure), green (vert), purple (pupure), black (sable). The two metals that are used are gold (or) and silver (argent). When they are represented by paint, gold is yellow and silver is white. Anything that is drawn or painted on the shield is called a charge. The basic charges are a broad, horizontal band across the middle of the shield (a fess), a narrower band (a bar), a vertical band down the centre of the shield (a pale), a diagonal band from dexter chief to sinister base (a band), a band in the opposite direction indicates illegitimacy, two bands slanting up from near the base and coming to a point in the chief (a chevron), a vertical line down the centre of the shield and a horizontal line across the middle (a cross), a cross made by two diagonal lines (a saltire).

Outcomes
The students can:
- Describe a coat of arms using some simple vocabulary used in heraldry.

A family tree

Richard Emmott = Jenet Hartley
1510–1550   1512–1560
(m.1530)

Thomas Emmott = Christabell Blakey 1531–1580 1533–1582 (m.1555)	**Marie** 1533–1536	**Lyonell** 1534–1535

Ellena   **Anna = Robert Savage**   **Roger**   **Lucia = Hugh Greenwood**
1557–1558   1558–1610   1558–1607   1559–1603   1562–1630   1560–1631
                      (m.1579)   (m.1580)

A family tree

Age range
- Years 3/4 (SP4/5).
- Years 5/6 (SP6/7).

Resources
Family trees of the Tudor royal family (optional).

Using the worksheet
The family tree here is fictitious but it is made using first names and surnames that were used in Tudor times. You may like to introduce this following the work on shields to show another way in which the ancestry of people can be investigated. You may use it after looking at the family tree of the Tudor royal family to show that the family tree of ordinary people can be worked out too. The worksheet can be used to develop number skills and to reveal a little of the lives of the people in the family.

Younger students
You may like to link this worksheet with **1 B** 'The Tudor timeline' and see in which monarch's reign the family tree belongs. You could then carry on linking the two together to find out in which monarch's reign other members of the family were born.

You could put these questions on the board for the students to answer.
1. How long did the following live – Richard Emmott, Thomas Emmott, Lucia Greenwood?
2. Do the life times follow a trend? Explain your answer.
3. How many people died in the first few years of life?

Answers
1. 40, 49, 68.
2. Yes. People who lived more recently lived longer than those who lived in the past.
3. 3.

You may use the answers from questions 2 and 3 to explore health issues in Tudor times.

Outcomes
The students can:
- Link a family tree to other events of the time.
- Perform calculations on the dates in a family tree.
- Identify and describe a trend in data.

Older students
The students could look at the link between this worksheet and **1 B** and discover the reigns in which marriages occur in the family. They may also look to see if the people have anything in common with the royal family such as being born or dying in the same year.

The students could answer the questions 1 to 3 then try these questions:
4. How old was Jenet Hartley when she gave birth to Thomas?
5. Did Richard and Jenet live long enough to see Thomas married?
6. Did Thomas and Christabell live long enough to see their children marry?
7. The students could use their imagination to add to the family tree. For this they may like to research records at the local library to find common first names for the seventeenth century. They may also like to look up the surnames of local families and see if they know anyone with those names today.

Answers
4. 19.
5. Richard did not live long enough but Jenet did.
6. Yes.

Outcomes
The students can:
- Extract information from a family tree.
- Perform calculations on the dates in a family tree.

The deserving poor

James Smith had rented a farm for a few years but the landlord decided that he wanted the farm for himself to raise sheep. James pleaded with the landlord to let his wife and children stay in the farm house while he looked for work. The landlord agreed and James set off across the countryside to find work. All he found were more people looking for work. Some were men on their own. Others were families. Most of the people had been farmers or worked on farms.

The people moved around the countryside in groups. Sometimes a day's work was found tending the gardens of a rich landowner. At other times no work was found and the people moved on. James decided to try his luck in a town. He was fortunate. Before he became a farmer, he was a cartwright and after walking through the town he found a cartwright needing an extra worker.

James brought his family to the town and they rented a room in a house. James's wife Susanna spun wool for a cloth maker next door. Her work provided more money to feed and clothe the family. James injured his back while working on a heavy cart. This meant that he could not work so his elder daughter, Marie, began spinning wool with her mother to help earn enough money to live.

After a while Susanna fell ill and could not work. James decided that he must beg for money and went to see the Justice of the Peace. James was considered to be a member of the deserving poor and the Justice of the Peace gave him a licence to beg.

In time, James's and Susanna's health improved and both could work again. When James's employer died, he took over the cartwright business and the Smith family moved into a house of their own.

1. The landlord discovered that he could make more money farming sheep than renting out his land to James. Was it fair to take James's home too? Explain your answer.

   ✎ ....

2. If you lived in the countryside and saw a large group of people moving about on your land, how would you feel?

   ✎ ....

3. Who else do you think could be considered the deserving poor?

   ✎ ....

4. What do you think might happen to someone who begged without a licence?

   ✎ ....

The deserving poor

Age range
- Years 3/4 (SP4/5).
- Years 5/6 (SP6/7).

Resources
A photocopy of the worksheet.

Using the worksheet
If you have been considering the rich in activities **3A** and **3B**, this activity gives an opportunity to consider the poor and some factors that accounted for their poverty. You may like to point out to the students that while we tend to think of all the Tudors being rich because most of the paintings we have from that time are of rich Tudors, most people were poor and few portraits were painted. Even when poor people were represented in art, they were sometimes made to appear better dressed than they actually were.

Younger students
The students should read through the account of James Smith and his family and work through the questions. They may need help in finding out what a cartwright (one who makes carts) and a Justice of the Peace (a magistrate) are. Question 1 could be addressed by the students working in small groups and then comparing their answers.

Possible answers
1. James only rented the farm so it was fair the farmer wanted it back. The farmer was unfair in that he did not help James find other work or accommodation.
2. Frightened. They are strangers and there are a large number of them. Angry. They have no right to be there.
3. Widows with children to support, people who are too ill to work, old people, orphans, soldiers and sailors who have been disabled in battles.
4. They would be punished.

Outcomes
The students know that:
- Using farmland for sheep led to some people becoming poor.
- Illness can contribute to poverty.
- There were rules for dealing with the poor.

Older students
Let the students try the whole of the worksheet. They may need to use secondary sources to find out what a cartwright and a Justice of the Peace were. You may, with sensitivity, explore what would happen to James and his family if they were alive today.

Outcomes
The students:
- Know that using farmland for sheep led to some people becoming poor.
- Know that illness can contribute to poverty.
- Know that there were rules for dealing with the poor.
- Can compare the care of the poor in Tudor times with the care of the poor today.

Spread ❸ (pages 8–9)

A land of small villages

The purpose of the spread

The purpose of this spread is to introduce the people at the beginning of Tudor times and give them a baseline to make comparisons with what happened later.

Background

The Tudor era began after a long period of bloody fighting and dispute. All manner of scales of war had left England impoverished when compared with her neighbours.

The purpose of this spread is to make it clear that England was backward in all sorts of ways at this time.

In particular it is important to see how little urbanisation had occurred. That England was insular and not in the mainstream of Europe. That most people lived in the countryside in poverty and in houses and shacks that were poor in quality. As a result, the majority have not survived.

The nature of feudal society could be described here, for it was still entrenched in English society, with large fields and the tithe system.

One thing that students may not realise is that, at this stage, England was still a forested country.

For hundreds of years before the Tudor times society in England had been organised according to the feudal system. This system was used all over Europe. The head of the society was the king. Below him were the dukes or barons. They were granted lands which they had to maintain and in return they had to support the king when battles were needed to be fought. Most of the people who lived on the lands of a baron were serfs – virtually his slaves. They had to work the fields and provide food for their master's court and, if they were lucky, for themselves, as well. Men who were fit had to serve in their master's armies and fight in his battles.

The Hundred Years War began in 1337 when Edward III, a Plantagenet king tried to claim the throne of France. The English won a number of battles including Crecy and Agincourt but in 1429 Joan of Arc led a successful counterattack. The war ended in 1429 when the English had lost all their possessions in France except Calais. Fighting extensive campaigns like this weakened the country. At the same time the plague occurred, ravaged the land and caused further weakening of village life.

In 1455 the Wars of the Roses began when two powerful Plantagenet families fought for the throne of England. Each family had a rose as an emblem. There was the red rose of the Lancastrians and the white rose of the Yorkists hence the name the war of the roses. Barons lined up with each family and fought their cause thus weakening village life still further. The Lancastrians won the war in 1485 and the Tudor times began.

Deserted villages

Many towns and villages that exist today also existed in Tudor times. Some however, no longer exist. The villages failed to survive because the people in them either moved away to find work or were killed by the plague. Evidence of the villages can still be seen in the landscape. Mounds of earth can be seen where houses once stood. By looking at the arrangement of the mounds archaeologists can work out the position of roads and build up a picture of what the village might have looked like.

Make a model of a deserted village in the following way.

1. Make a collection of small boxes such as used milk cartons. These can represent houses. You could also collect empty match boxes or even small round boxes which could be used to represent sheds.

2. Make an arrangement of the boxes to represent the remains of the buildings in the village then cover them with a green towel. Make sure that all the "remains" of the buildings can be seen as mounds in the towel.

3. Give your model to a friend and ask them to work out the arrangement of the buildings and the likely positions of roads and paths.

4. Let your friend make a drawing of what your village may have looked like here:

5. Remove the towel and compare the arrangement of the buildings in the picture with the arrangements of the boxes.

Deserted villages

Age range
- Years 3/4 (SP4/5).
- Years 5/6 (SP6/7).

Resources
A collection of small boxes such as empty milk cartons from the infant department, empty match boxes and small circular boxes. Older students will need secondary sources featuring photographs of deserted village sites.

Using the worksheet
Later in the book the students will learn about the effects of changes in land use and the effects of the plague on village life. You may introduce these factors simply here then ask the children what might happen when a village was deserted. Look for answers about the buildings falling into ruin. Timbers rotting away but the outline of the foundations may be left in the earth. You may also like to point out that ground which is regularly used as a path or a road is worn away and if appropriate show where paths have developed around the edges of the school field. Tell the students that historians may study ancient maps or read accounts that suggest that a village once existed in a place, then archaeologists visit it and study the features on the ground which suggest a village was once present there.

Younger students
The students may work in pairs to make a village then give it to another pair of students to interpret.

Outcomes
The students:
- Know that villages were sometimes deserted but evidence was left in the landscape.
- Can work together to construct a model.
- Can interpret a model landscape.

Older students
Each student may make a collection of boxes. Often the only stone building in the village was the church and the foundations or even more of the building may still be seen. The students could mark out with pebbles the foundation of a church. When each student has interpreted the model of the friend, they can look at photographs in secondary sources about deserted villages.

Outcomes
The students:
- Know that villages were sometimes deserted but evidence was left in the landscape.
- Can interpret a model landscape.
- Can compare their models with photographic evidence from real deserted villages.

Field walking

When archaeologists visit some sites, they begin their investigations by field walking. This is usually done in ploughed fields in winter before the crops grow. In this exercise you can use the school field covered in grass but remember that in real field walking the bare earth is examined. When archaeologists field walk, they move slowly forwards looking at the ground for any unusual objects.

Prepare an area of ground for a friend to field walk in the following way.

1. Make a collection of small items such as coins, small pieces of pottery (without sharp edges).

2. Set out the items in the grass. Make a note of where you have put them.

3. Ask your friend to search the area and collect each item in a plastic bag and note where they found it.

4. When your friend has finished, compare their notes with yours and answer these questions:

   a) How observant was your friend? ✎ ....

   b) Explain your answer.

   ✎ ....

   ✎ ....

   c) Did your friend make an accurate record of where the items were found?

   ✎ ....

   d) Explain your answer.

   ✎ ....

   ✎ ....

Field walking

Age range

- Years 3/4 (SP4/5).
- Years 5/6 (SP6/7).

Resources

Access to the school field or any area which has not been fouled by dogs. Small metal objects such as coins, nails, buckles, buttons, small pieces of pottery without sharp edges.

Using the worksheet

When fields are ploughed, the soil is turned over. Items that became buried long ago can be brought to the surface through the action of ploughing. Even if the item is in a clod of earth, over the winter the weather can erode the clod and the item can be exposed. Archaeologists examine a field in a systematic way. They make a map of the field using ranging poles then they walk slowly in a line across the field. If something is found it is collected and its position is marked on a map. You do not need to tell the students about this when introducing the activity but when discrepancies show up in the collection of the items, you may encourage the students to think how they could improve the way they collect items and this may lead them to think about map making.

Younger students

The students may work in pairs. Each pair setting out an area of the field (perhaps four metres wide by twenty metres long) for another pair to work.

Outcomes

The students:
- Know that field walking can be used to collect archaeological evidence.
- Can make careful observations.
- Can record their findings.

Older students

The students could work in pairs and perhaps use a larger area than the younger students. They could perhaps group items together so that they could be interpreted. For example a few coins together may suggest that a purse had been buried, some broken pieces of pottery in one area may suggest that a kitchen may have been buried under the ground.

Outcomes

The students:
- Know that field walking can be used to collect archaeological evidence.
- Can record their findings.
- Can attempt to interpret their findings.

Spread 4 (pages 10–11)

Our village in 1500

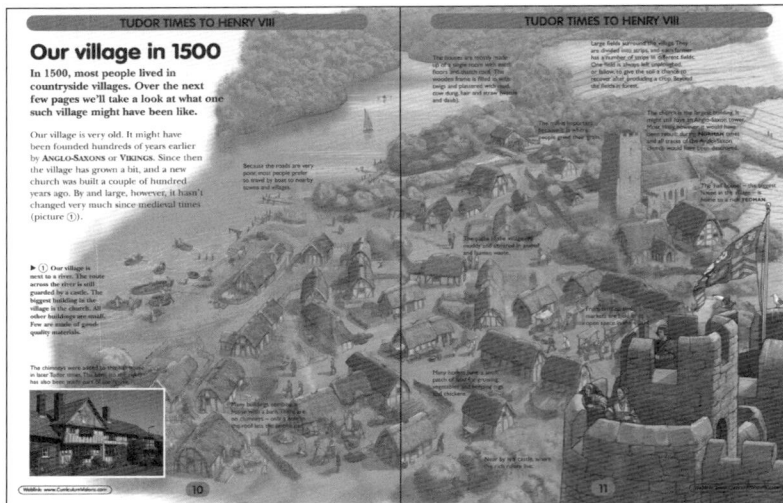

The purpose of the spread

This spread concentrates on the way a countryside village might have looked in about 1500, near the start of Tudor times.

Students will need to look at it carefully to pick up the main points.

The village may have had a track. This might have been close to the stream but more likely would have been a little uphill, unless the floodplain was wide.

Most village sites are on slightly higher land, for flooding was a problem.

Houses will not have been planned and so are scattered about in what might appear to be a random fashion. We get some idea of this when we see old houses that have been preserved and find their orientation does not readily fit in with the road plan of today. It's not that the road plan has changed, it's that when roads were not important, the need to be located beside one was not there.

Many of the better off people in a village would have had a large garden in which they could grow their own vegetables and perhaps keep animals. As a result, the village would have seemed quite open, not a collection of buildings side by side.

The village consisted of people with more money and those who were poor and simply worked on the land as labourers, relying on the lord to allow them to keep working their strips in the common fields. These people had no money to improve their homes and they were of the simplest kind. Many could not afford to get the land on which to build and so they rented their shacks from the better off.

This is an important point, because parts of a village where the shacks were would have looked much more rundown than the places where the better off lived.

The road was a muddy track. It was used only for local traffic and was pitted and the holes filled with mud and water.

There was no sanitation of any kind and so both human and animal waste would have marred the scene and added to the village aroma.

Notice that the wealthier have plastered walls to their houses while the poor simply have mud, straw and dung walls that would have been a pale brown colour. Any exposed beams would have been natural wood – silver brown.

Students should also notice that the houses have either no windows or very small windows because glass was not available for windows. Windows would all have had shutters to keep out the cold.

What we will do is to use this as a baseline on which to see changes over the following century.

Make a simple timber frame

1. Take two lolly sticks and lay them on the table as figure 1 shows.

2. Use sticky tape to stick them together at A.

3. Repeat steps 1 and 2 with two more lolly sticks.

4. Hang the lolly sticks over the edge of a table as shown in figure 2 and stick two more lolly sticks to them at B, C, D and E.

Figure 1

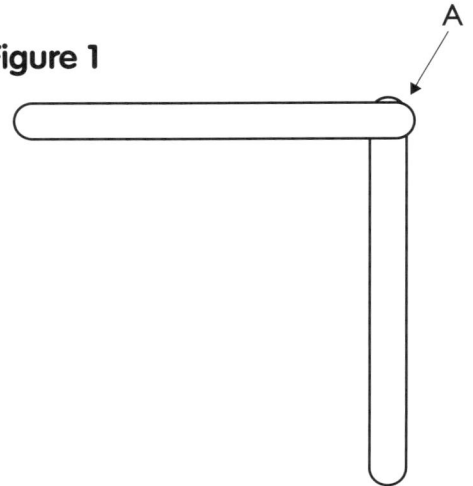

Figure 2

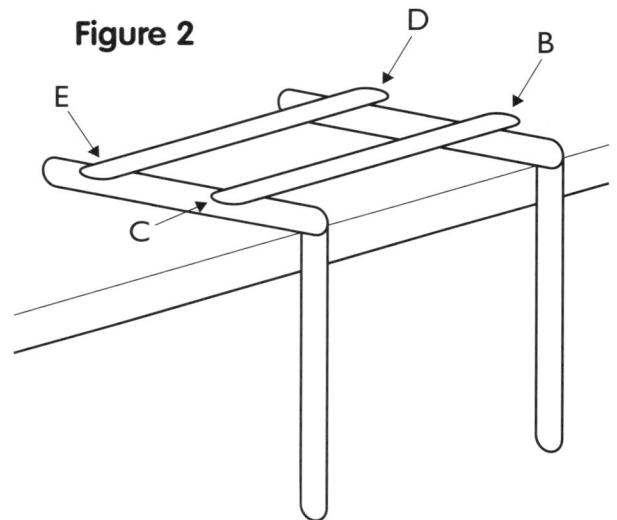

5. Stand the frame up and stick two more lolly sticks to the frame at F, G, H and J.

Figure 3

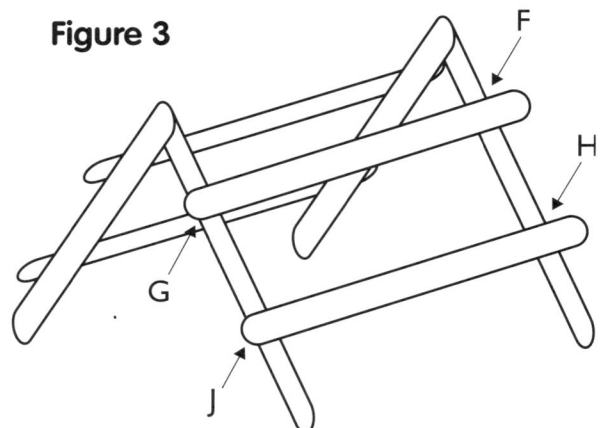

6. You may cut out pieces of card and stick them to the frame to make a simple model house.

Make a simple timber frame

Age range
- Years 3/4 (SP4/5).
- Years 5/6 (SP6/7).

Resources
To make one timber frame house you need six lolly sticks, sticky paper and scissors. Card (you may like to tear open some corrugated cardboard as this produces the effect of wood poles attached to the frame).

Using the worksheet
There was a law that if you could start building a house in the morning and finish it and have a fire burning in the hearth by evening you could own your house and live in it. You could use this information to introduce the worksheet. Tell the students that they are members of the deserving poor who have arrived on the outskirts of a village and have to produce their houses quickly if they are going to be allowed to stay there. The worksheet also introduces the students to the concept of a timber frame in a very simple way. It does not matter if there are bits of sticky paper on various parts of the frame the idea is to assemble the frame quickly. You may like to link this activity to activity **5** 'Wattle and daub' and activity **13B** 'Make a house'.

Younger students
The students may need help balancing the lolly sticks in figure 2. They may find it easier to work in pairs. They could put their houses together to make a village when they have finished.

Outcomes
The students can:
- Construct a simple timber frame.

Older students
The students may like to work individually and have a race to see who can build their house in the quickest time. Perhaps a rule could be set that only the owners of the first ten houses to be built can stay in the village and live there.

Outcomes
The students can:
- Construct a simple timber frame.

Spread ⑤ (pages 12–13)

Homes in the village

The purpose of the spread

This spread looks inside a home and considers the materials used for home making. It could be useful to compare present day homes with the homes featured here. The students should notice that many features we take for granted in modern homes just did not exist in early Tudor times for most people. Walls were not made of brick or concrete but woven sticks coated with mud and dung. There was no wallpaper on the inside and no paint. Windows were not present in the poorest homes and cooking was done on a hearth which was little more than an indoor camp fire. The rich began to have fireplaces and chimneys built into their new homes but the poor had to make do with a hole in the roof. The students should use this spread to build up the concept of home life.

Background

Here is some information which the students can use to help them compare life in an early Tudor home with a typical home today.

There is no alarm clock to wake you up. The crowing of a cockerel outside would be enough to end your sleep. You would probably live in one room with the fire in the centre. The fire was started by building a small pile of very small thin twigs, placing some very dry straw or paper next to it to act as tinder and then striking a piece of flint on a steel to make sparks. The flint and steel would have to be struck so that the sparks landed on the tinder. Some of them would be hot enough to make the tinder burst into flame and when this happened the small pieces of wood were placed very close so that they could catch fire too. Large pieces of wood could be put on the fire once the small pieces of wood were burning well.

Breakfast for poor people might be a cup of ale and a piece of bread then they would go straight out to work in the fields.

At the end of the day a hot meal may be taken. This would probably just be a kind of vegetable broth but if the household had been very lucky and managed to buy some meat this would have been added to the pot too.

Once daylight faded people went to bed.

In the houses of those with a little more money candles may be used at night. The cheapest candles were made from tallow (animal fats) and produced smoke and a foul smell as they burned. More expensive candles were made from beeswax and burned with a pleasant smell without smoke. You may like to show the students a beeswax candle available today and light it.

While we may think the poorest people were permanently dirty those a little richer were not much cleaner. If they had stone floors they would strew it with herbs which released a pleasant smell as people walked on them. After a while they would have to be swept up and replaced. Clothes and blankets got a regular clean but this may only take place about four times a year when they were washed in the river with home made soap (a mixture of animal fat, quicklime and ash).

Wattle and daub

1. Stick four long matchsticks in a piece of oasis as figure 1 shows.

2. Take a piece of straw that has been cut in half and thread it through the matchsticks as figure 2 shows.

3. Take another piece of straw and thread it through the matchsticks as figure 3 shows.

4. Repeat steps 2 and 3 until you have ten straws woven between the matchsticks.

5. Mix some flour and water to make a paste and daub it on the straws as figure 4 shows.

6. Leave for a few minutes to see if the paste drips off the straws. If it does, make a thicker paste. Coat your paste over the straws.

7. Leave overnight to let the paste set.

Figure 1

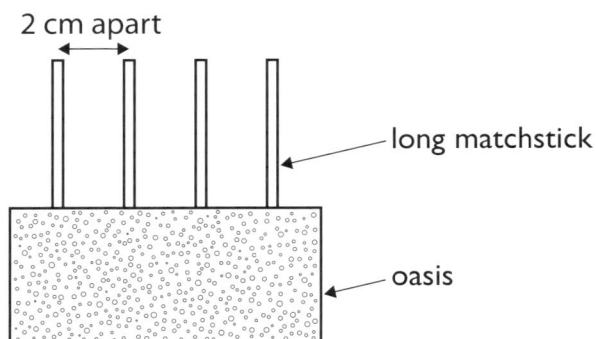

2 cm apart

long matchstick

oasis

Figure 2

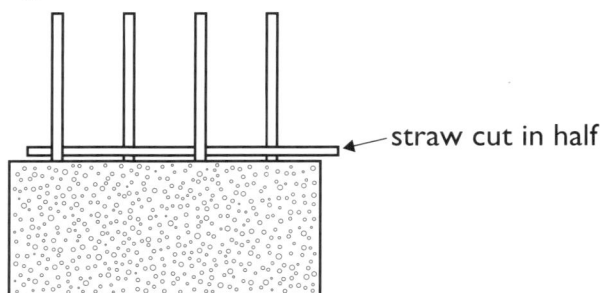

straw cut in half

Figure 3

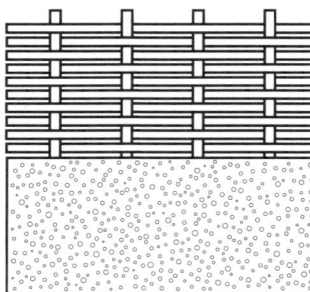

Figure 4

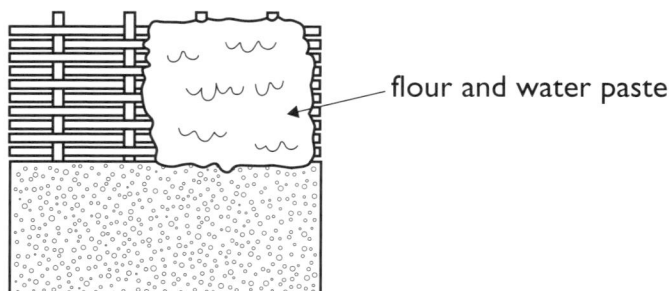

flour and water paste

Wattle and daub

Age range
- Years 3/4 (SP4/5).
- Years 5/6 (SP6/7).

Resources
For each group you need a piece of oasis about 8 cm across. Four long matches with their heads cut off, five straws cut in half lengthways (you may like to prepare these before the lesson), flour, water, a bowl, a spoon.

Using the worksheet
If you have done activity **4** you may like to remind the students and say that in many timber framed houses the gaps between the timbers were filled with wattle and daub. This was made by weaving small branches of hazel together and covering them with a mixture of clay, dung and horsehair. This mixture was then coated with a thin layer of plaster. Tell the students that they are going to make a piece of wattle and daub but instead of hazel branches they will be using matchsticks and straws and instead of clay, dung and horsehair they will be using flour and water. You may like to link this activity to **9A** 'Make a leaded window' and **13B** 'Make a house".

Younger students
The students may need to make sure that they sink the matchsticks about one and a half centimetres into the oasis. They should not pull the matchsticks from side to side as this will make the holes larger and the sticks will wobble. They may need help following the weaving pattern. They may need reassuring that if a matchstick does lean when a piece of straw is added it may lean back again when a second piece of straw is added. Care may be needed when making the flour paste. You may like to make some up for the students to use. It should be quite thick so that all of it does not flow off the straws and onto the oasis.

Outcomes
The students:
- Know how wattle and daub was made in Tudor times.
- Can follow instructions to make a model.
- Can make a piece of wattle and daub that does not have any gaps in it.

Older students
The students may wonder why the straws have to be split. The tension in full straws can pull the matchsticks out of place so cutting them lengthways and using half straws reduces this tension and keeps the matchsticks upright. The students may like to work in groups or individually.

Outcomes
The students:
- Know how wattle and daub was made in Tudor times.
- Can make a piece of wattle and daub that does not have any gaps in it.

Spread ⑥ (pages 14–15)

Village life

The purpose of the spread

This spread looks at some of the public buildings as these give an insight into the way in which life worked at the time.

Background

Again, the emphasis is on small scale and modest structures. Students may think of a hall as an important building, but it was not so in these times. It was more like a parish room we have in today's villages.

The building was not used for social functions, but as the place from which the steward and the bailiff operated. It was the place for collecting taxes and the place where rough justice was meted out and fines collected.

The village hall should be contrasted with the village church. This was far and away the most important building in the village. In other villages where the lord of the manor lived nearby, the church may have been located close to the manor house for the convenience of the lord, who would have had his own private entrance, chapel and pews, often screened off completely from the view of the villagers.

The church would have been made of stone. We have enough old churches remaining for the shape and structure of such buildings to be seen by students on half day field trips.

In general it was one large room. It would have been brightly painted inside because, in 1500, the church was Catholic. There would have been many statues of saints and the whole service would have been in Latin. The villagers would not have been able to read English, so making a Bible available to them would not necessarily have helped. But keep in mind that one element of the reformation was to put a Bible in English into every church, implying that the literacy of the better off was substantial.

At this time, the instructions of how to conduct life came from the priest. After it was possible for parishioners to read the Bible for themselves, this would not have been any longer entirely true, resulting in a fundamental shift in society.

But above all, the church would not have been a silent place of tidy pews. It would have been quite open, with the floor strewn with straw. Animals were sometimes kept in the church. Also, if the sermon was long, the straw helped to soak up the results of people being kept from attending to their personal needs elsewhere.

The market is an embryonic feature of the village. Markets imply surplus and the money to buy it. At the start of Tudor times this was limited. But it was different from what had gone on before. Local food items were now on sale. Also markets were not confined to the annual fairs of travelling peddlers that had prevailed in medieval times.

People in general were still forthright in their treatment of wrongdoers. Pillories and stocks were a feature of a marketplace. Here vagrants and wrongdoers could be displayed and be subject to ridicule and pelting with anything people could get to hand. Much of it was not nice. Being put in the pillories or stocks was not meant to be a soft option.

Notice the reference to looking after the parish poor. At this stage this would have been more the responsibility of the church than it was after the reformation. But no one wanted the poor from outside to add to their burden.

Beggars and thieves

People who were fit enough to work but did not were called sturdy rogues. Some simply could not find work but others preferred to beg or steal instead.

Beggars

Abraham man – a beggar who appears to be mad. He dresses in tatty clothes and dances about. He says things that do not make sense.

Palliard – a beggar who appears to be covered in sores and is very ill. The sores are made by sticking irritants to the skin such as the plants called crowfoot and spearwort. A palliard also puts blood and dirt on their skin and clothes. They add more as the blood and dirt wear off.

Ruffler – a beggar who tells a sad story about himself. He may say something like this "Please listen, sir, I am in need. I have tried my best in the war and fought hard for my Queen but I was very unlucky. I was cut with a sword on my left arm, side and leg. Oh the pain, it hurts just to tell you. Oh the pain, sir. Folks say I am lucky to be alive but now I'm not so sure with all this pain, sir."

Thieves

Angler (or hooker) – a thief who has a hook on the end of a long pole. It can be poked through open windows to steal objects from inside houses.

Cut purse – purses were hung from a belt by a cord. A cut purse used a knife to cut the cord and take the purse when the victim was looking the other way.

Highway robber – a thief who stands in front of a person travelling on the highway and demands money.

Pick pocket – a thief who dips their hand into a person's pocket while the person is looking the other way.

1. Write something that you think an Abraham man might say.

   ✎ ....

2. Write something that a palliard might say.

   ✎ ....

3. How could a person be made to look away so a cut purse could work?

   ✎ ....

4. Imagine you are a judge at a court. These are the punishments you can give: whipping, burning a hole in the ear, placing in the stocks, branding with a hot iron, cutting off a hand, hanging.

   What punishment would you give to (i) an Abraham man? ✎ ....

   (ii) a ruffler? ✎ .... (iii) an angler? ✎ ....

   (iv) a highway robber? ✎ .... (v) a pickpocket? ✎ ....

50

Beggars and thieves

Age range
- Years 3/4 (SP4/5).
- Years 5/6 (SP6/7).

Resources
Copies of the worksheet. For younger students – a long pole with a plastic hook stuck on one end (optional). For older students – ragged clothes, jam (optional).

Using the worksheet
If the students have done activity **2E** about 'The deserving poor' you may like to remind them of it. This activity deals with the undeserving poor. These are people who are fit to work but do not by their own choice. It should be mentioned that some people who were fit but did not work simply could not find work but many wealthy Tudors thought that they were lazy which was not the case.

Younger students
Let the students work through the sheet. You may like to have some groups of students showing how a pickpocket could work. The class could decide the fate of the thieves in question 4 by a show of hands. Some students could try and use a long pole for angling an object off a table.

Outcomes
The students:
- Know about the range of tricks used by beggars in Tudor times.
- Know about some of the different kinds of thieves in Tudor times.
- Can make a judgement about the punishment of crimes.

Older students
The students can work through the sheet. Some of the more theatrically minded students may like to perform their answers to the rest of the class. Ragged clothes could be worn and perhaps some jam could be used as blood for the palliard. The students could answer question 4 on their own and then discuss their judgements.

Outcomes
The students:
- Know about the range of tricks used by beggars in Tudor times.
- Know about some of the different kinds of thieves in Tudor times.
- Can evaluate judgements made by different people.

Money

The main coins of the Tudor age were pounds, shillings and pennies.

The symbol for a pound is '£'. The symbol for a shilling is 's'. The symbol for a penny is 'd' (from the Roman coin 'denarius'). The sum of ten pounds, five shillings and six pence was written:

£10 5s 6d.

If there was a list of items and their value, the symbols could be written as column headings as this example shows:

	£	s	d
30 sheep	3	8	4
12 lambs	1	2	10

Twelve pennies were worth a shilling and twenty shillings were worth a pound.

There were also other coins. These were half pennies and quarter pennies, a groat (worth four pennies) and a mark (worth 160 pennies).

1. How many groats are there in (i) a shilling? ✎ ....

   (ii) a pound? ✎ ....

2. What is thirty pennies in shillings and pence?   s .... d ....

3. What is 45 shillings in pounds and shillings?   £ .... s ....

4. What is 608 pennies in pounds, shillings and pence? £ .... s .... d ....

5. Add these two amounts together   £ s d

                                               3 2 4

                                               4 5 5

6. Take away the bottom amount from the top amount   £ s d

                                              6 10 6

                                              2 4 2

Money

Age range
- Years 3/4 (SP4/5).
- Years 5/6 (SP6/7).

Resources
Copies of the worksheet.

Using the worksheet
You may like to introduce this activity when looking at the text on rents or the market on the spread in the student book.

Younger students
The students can work through the whole of the sheet. If appropriate they could also try the work for the older students set out below.

Answers
1. (i) 3, (ii) 60.
2. Two shillings and six pence (2s 6d).
3. Two pounds, five shillings (£2 5s 0d).
4. Two pounds, ten shillings and eight pence. (£2 10s 8d).
5. £7 7s 9d.
6. £4 6s 4d.

Outcomes
The students:
- Know the money used in Tudor times.
- Can make simple calculations in pounds, shillings and pence.

Older students
The students can work through the whole of the sheet and then try these examples which you may like to put on the board:

1. Add £2 5s 3d to £31 8s 10d
   (answer £33 14s 1d).
2. Take away £2 6s 0d from £5 0s 0d
   (answer £2 14s 0d).

3. Multiply £5 4s 0d by 3 (answer £15 12s 0d).
4. Multiply £8 12s 3d by 5 (answer £43 1s 3d)
5. Divide £10 4s 8d by 2 (answer (£5 2s 4d).
6. Divide £10 1s 9d by 3 (answer £3 7s 3d

You may also like to try this role play activity. It could be used as part of a Tudor day when the children are dressed up in costume.

Nicholas Parker left a will. It was to be read out by a lawyer when his four children were sat with pen a paper. Whoever made the fastest calculation when the lawyer had finished could have his horse as well as some money. The lawyer reads out:

"I, Nicholas Parker, let my four children have an equal share of my money which is £60 13s 8d. The children must then calculate four equal shares and the first to finish wins the horse."
(answer £15 3s 5d)

Outcomes
The students can:
- Know the money used in Tudor times.
- Make calculations in pounds, shillings and pence.

Spell as you like

In Tudor times you could spell the words as they sound to you. This meant that there could be many spellings for the same word.

1. Here are some words from Tudor times. They are taken from a list of a man's possessions. What do you think the items are?

   A silver spone

   Three panes

   Four poetts

   Five qwsines

   A peece of woolen clothe

   A maire and two fyles

2. You could also spell your name anyway you like. Spell your name in different ways in the space below.

   ....

3. Write a letter to a friend spelling as you like. How quickly can your friend read and understand it? You may like to start your letter writing the date as they did in Tudor times. The date of the month is given but the year is worked out from the date when the monarch came to the throne. For example, the 11th of May 1514 would be written:

   The eleventh day of May in the fifth year of the reign of our sovereign Lord Henry VIII by the grace of God.

   Elizabeth II came to the throne in 1953. How would you write today's date Tudor style?

   ....

Spell as you like

Age range

- Years 3/4 (SP4/5) but omit the phrase.
- Years 5/6 (SP6/7).

Resources

A copy of the worksheet.

Using the worksheet

Having spent time helping the students to spell properly you may be reluctant to let them spell as they like. However, this activity helps them to appreciate why old documents that they may use as evidence have many different spellings for the same thing.

Younger students

These students can work through parts 1 and 2 although they may like to write a few sentences with Tudor style spellings.

Answers

A silver spoon, three pans, four pots, five cushions, a piece of woollen cloth, a mare and two foals.

Outcomes

The students know that:
- Words could be spelled in many different ways.
- Writers spelled the words according to how they thought the words sounded.

Older students

The students can work through all three parts of the worksheet. They may like to write the letter to a friend using the letters shown on worksheet **6D** to make the document look like an authentic Tudor letter. The last activity can be extended by the friend writing back.

Outcomes

The students:
- Know that words can be spelled phonetically in many different ways.
- Can communicate using the spellings of Tudor times.

Writing the Tudor way

Many Tudors wrote in a style of hand writing known as secretary. Here are the capital letters and small letters in the secretary style.

You can use the capitals in sentences for the names of things as we do today but you can also use a capital letter to begin any word that you think is important. Note that capital F is a double f.

| A | B | C | D | E | F | G | H | I and J | K | L | M |

| N | O | P | Q | R | S | T | U and V | W | X | Y | Z |

| a | b | c | d | e | f | g | h | i and j | k | l | m |

| n | o | p | q | r | s | t | u | v | w | x | y | z |

Writing the Tudor way

Age range
- Years 3/4 (SP4/5).
- Years 5/6 (SP6/7).

Resources
Copies of the worksheet.

Using the worksheet
This activity links to activity **6c** 'Spell as you like'. You may like to remind the students of this when you issue the worksheet. You may introduce the worksheet after the students have read about the activities in the hall in the village and say that we know about some of these activities through written documents. These documents are written in a different style to the one we use today.

Younger students
Challenge the students to write their names in the secretary style. They could also write about the meal they plan to eat at lunchtime or the meal they have just eaten. They can pass their work among their friends and see if it can be read and understood by others. The students may spell as they like to make their work more like the Tudor style.

Outcomes
The students can:
- Write in the style used by many Tudors.
- Read words written in the secretary style.

Older students
You may tell the students that activities such as paying rents or recording punishments were written down and these written documents can be used as evidence in finding out about the past. Many Tudors used a style of writing called secretary and in this activity the students are going to write a letter in this style. They could date the letter as shown in activity **6c** and spell as they like too. They can pass their work among their friends and see if it can be read and understood by others.

Outcomes
The students can:
- Write a letter in the style used by many Tudors.
- Read a letter written in the secretary style.

Spread **7** (pages 16–17)

Farmland changes

The purpose of the spread

This spread begins to introduce students to the idea of land reform. It only began in Tudor times and did not cover the whole country at this early stage. But its effects were profound, both for peasants and yeomen.

Background

This spread allows you to introduce the idea of land tenure. Students should be able to see that land was owned by a few people. Most of the land was owned by a very few wealthy people or organisations like the church. Some of the land was owned freehold by yeomen. The peasants had no land.

Although change of tenure was only begun in Tudor times, we will assume our village is at the forefront of this change. It is vital to an understanding of the whole way in which the countryside works today.

In the days before consolidation of holdings there was no point living in a house in the fields. Your field strips were widely scattered and so you lived in a village. But once land had been consolidated you could go and live in a farmhouse in your fields. This applied to yeomen as much as it did to the people buying church land from Henry after the reformation. It explains why these are the oldest houses we find out in the countryside and why older houses were all in villages or towns.

The movement worked in two directions. In terms of numbers of people, the greatest movement was from the villages to the towns and that was mainly by peasants who had been dispossessed of the right to farm any land. Enclosed land was much more efficient to farm than open field land and needed fewer people. Profits from farmland therefore went up for those who owned the land, but jobs for the peasants went down.

This is, in part, responsible for the number of people wandering across the countryside and of which we will find out more later.

The flow of wealth to the countryside happened when the king released church land for sale. New town people came out to the countryside where the highest possible status was to have a house surrounded by your own land.

Note that the events of this spread cover the whole Tudor period and in part rely on events that happen at a specific date as outlined by the next spread.

Can you understand these rogues?

Some of the people who roamed the countryside were criminals. They were called rogues. They had their own terms for many things so it was difficult for ordinary people to know what they were talking about. Here are two rogues having a discussion.

Rowland "Edmund was a foist. He had been drawing in the market all morning then he decides to do a lift. The trouble was, by then he had been to the boozing ken and didn't have his glaziers about him and was up before the beak in no time".

Archie "Did you get a snap?"

Rowland "No! Stow you. Its darkmans and I need to couch a hogshead. I'm goujng to dream about a cony with a full bung or a prancer that is easy to prig".

Archie "Don't try it though or it will be the chats for you".

Here are the words that the rogues used to stop people understanding them. Can you work out what they said – only one option is right.

foist – (a) lookout, (b) a pickpocket.

drawing – (a) picking pockets, (b) pulling something along.

lift – (a) steal from a shop, (b) carry someone around.

boozing ken (a) the town drunk, (b) an ale house.

glaziers – (a) glassworkers, (b) eyes.

beak – (a) magistrate, (b) shopkeeper.

snap – (a) share of stolen goods, (b) a light meal.

stow you (a) pack up your things, (b) be quiet.

darkmans (a) night, (b) gloomy person.

couch a hogshead – (a) kill a pig, (b) have a sleep.

cony – (a) a rabbit, (b) a person easy to rob.

bung – (a) a type of cork, (b) a purse.

prance – (a) horse, (b) clown.

prig – (a) steal, (b) stab.

chats – (a) talkative people, (b) gallows.

Can you understand these rogues?

Age range

- Years 3/4 (SP4/5).
- Years 5/6 (SP6/7).

Resources

Copies of the worksheets.

Using the worksheet

If the students have done activity **2E** about 'The deserving poor' and activity **6A** about 'Beggars and thieves' you may like to remind them of them now. The three activities link together to give a picture of what life was like in the countryside. There were large numbers of people wandering around looking for work but some of their number had decided that it was easier to live as criminals and to protect themselves if they had their own language.

Younger students

The students can work through the worksheet. The answers are: foist – (b) pickpocket; drawing – (a) picking pockets; lift – (a) steal from a shop; boozing ken – (b) an ale house; glaziers – (b) eyes; beak – (a) magistrate; snap – (a) share of stolen goods; stow you – (b) be quiet; darkmans – (a) night; couch a hogshead – (b) have a sleep; cony – (b) person easy to rob; bung – (b) purse; prancer – (a) horse; prig – (a) steal; chats – (b) gallows.

You may like to divide the class into groups and let each group work out its own simple language, write a short piece using its vocabulary then challenge other groups to work out what has been written.

Outcomes

The students:
- Know rogues had their own language.
- Can decipher a conversation between two rogues.

Older students

The students can work through the worksheet. The answers are given in the section for younger students above. The students could try and write another piece using the words on the worksheet and some extra words here. They are cove (a man), mort (a woman), autem mort (woman thief who steals clothes left hanging out to dry), walking mort or doxy (woman tramp), greenmans (fields), peck (food), stamps (legs).

Outcomes

The students can:
- Decipher a conversation between two rogues.
- Construct a piece of writing using the rogues language.

Spread **8** (pages 18–19)

Our town in 1500

The purpose of the spread

We have now introduced students to the detail of a village. Here we begin to look at a town.

Background

The difficulty of talking about a town in 1500 will be that so little of it appears to be left. One of the best ways of seeing into the past for towns is to use a historic map. There are town maps dating back to the early 19th century and before, and if you can get hold of local versions of these then you will see just how much land was allocated to each town house. It is all of this land that was subsequently filled in.

Remind students that people in the early 16th century were fairly self-contained. So town houses had market gardens. They also needed places to keep animals.

This might be a good moment to discuss the needs of animals. Until the days of industrialisation and mechanisation, animals were the main source of both power and transport. But they needed to be fed. Keeping animals meant devoting farmland to providing their food. A fifth to a quarter of all land was used just to feed animals.

In a town, people had to buy animal feedstuff from people in the countryside or have enough land in the town to grow their own. As it was not possible to have large areas of land in a town, feedstuffs would be brought in by cart on a regular basis. It is also worth telling students that this happened as recently as the first half of the twentieth century when, in the days before refrigeration, cows were still kept in city dairies and milkmen and rag and bone men still made their rounds using carts drawn by horses.

Just like the village, the houses at this time were not particularly substantial. Multiple storeys would come later. But there was a definite hierarchy of location. The more wealthy you were, the better the place you could afford to choose in the town. In our example, it is proximity to the abbey gates and the market.

So in a town the wealthiest would be nearest the middle and the poorest on the margins. The wealthiest of all, of course, were not in towns, but in the country as wealth and land went together. This is a pattern that has existed through time.

Even in places like London, famous urban roads like the Strand were, at this time, like being in the country, with the wealthy having palaces in their own grounds lining the route between the city and Westminster.

What is also worthy of note is the range of town trades. These are still operating in what effectively is a guild system, but they include trades like tailors not found in villages.

Make a pomander

1. Select an orange that has a stalk. It should also be ripe and have a thin skin.

2. Tie one end of a piece of string to the stalk. You will use this later to hang up the pomander.

3. Begin sticking cloves into the orange around the stalk.

4. Continue sticking cloves in around the orange until the whole of the orange is covered.

5. Place two teaspoons of ground cinnamon in a bowl and roll the orange in it.

6. Press the orange into the powder so that the powder sticks to it.

7. Wrap the orange in tissue paper and keep in a dark cupboard for two to three weeks.

8. Take out the pomander and hang it up.

Make a pomander

1. Selekte an orange that haz a stalke. It shuld also be rype and have a thyne skyne.

2. Ty wone ende of a strynge to thee stalke. You will use this layter to hange up thee pomander.

3. Beginne stickinge cloves into thee orange arownde the stalke.

4. Continue sticking cloves in arownde thee orange until the hole of thee orange is coved.

5. Place too teaespones of growd cinnamon on a bowel and rolle thee orange in it.

6. Pres thee orange into thee powder so that theepowder stickess to it.

7. Rap thee orange in tishoo payper and keepe in a darke cubord fore too to three weekes.

8. Take out thee pomander and hange it up.

Make a pomander

Age range

- With years 3/4 (SP4/5) you may wish to issue the worksheet as a homework a few weeks before you begin work on the Tudors so that they will be ready for use in class or around school. Alternatively, you could issue the work sheet as you work through the Tudors so that it is ready towards the end of the study.
- With years 5/6 (SP6/7) you may wish to issue the worksheet a few weeks before you begin work on Tudors. Alternatively you could issue the worksheet as you work through the Tudors so that it is ready towards the end of the study.

Resources

A copy of the worksheet. If done in school thin skinned oranges, string, cloves, cinnamon, teaspoons, bowls and tissue paper will be needed. Secondary sources about pomanders (optional for older students)

Using the worksheet

You may wish to use the worksheet before you start work on Tudors so the pomanders can be ready to provide an authentic smell to the classroom. Alternatively you may introduce it when the students have been considering smells in a Tudor settlement. If you have done worksheet **6c** about spelling you may like to use the lower half of the worksheet and let the students translate the instructions. If you do not wish to use the Tudor style spellings use the top part of the worksheet.

Younger students

Issue the worksheet and let the students work in groups to translate the instructions and make the pomander.

Outcomes

The students can:
- Follow instructions to make a pomander.
- Work together safely on a project.

Older students

The students can work individually or in pairs. They could use secondary sources to find out about how pomanders evolved into a perforated sphere of material for holding fragrant substances.

Outcomes

The students can:
- Follow instructions to make a pomander.
- Use secondary sources to find out more about pomanders.

Spread ❾ (pages 20–21)

The great Tudor houses

The purpose of the spread

To show the nature of life for the rich.

Background

Tudor houses are some of the most obvious signs of wealth but also of fashion.

The important idea is to see that the Tudors experimented with a brand new way of living. A field trip to any castle will show that it is a cold, empty place, designed with protection in mind and with little attention being given to comfort.

Many castles were converted in Tudor times, so the old halls may have had floors added and the rooms each given a chimney. These would not have been features of a medieval castle.

Older buildings were also poorly lit because windows were small as glass was not readily available. With an increase in the amount of glass, windows could be made larger. Of course, glass could not be made in large sheets and so the design of windows to some extent reflects this, with mullions and transoms dividing the frame up into smaller pieces. Even so lead had to be used as it had been in churches – to fix small pieces of glass together in a decorative pattern. Leaded windows were therefore a response to technology.

But the many new grand buildings of Tudor times did not need to make alterations to older buildings. They did not need the defensive structures and any crenulation was purely for decorative reasons. Thus fabulous palaces such as Hampton Court could be designed in a new and revolutionary way.

Of particular note is the use of wood as panelling and floorboarding. This made the homes much warmer and was made possible with the use of fireplaces that reduced the risk of open fires getting out of control.

Students could also be introduced to the way in which the wealthy lived in the city. Some still had palaces, but most had town houses and these went up over several floors because a town or city has less ground space than would be available in the country.

Make a leaded window

Figure 1

1. Cut out two strips of cardboard 18 cm long and 3 cm wide.

2. Cut out two strips of cardboard 17 cm long and 3 cm wide.

3. Set out the strips as figure 1 shows and stick them together with sticky paper. This is the window frame.

18 cm x 3 cm

17 cm x 3 cm

Cardboard strips

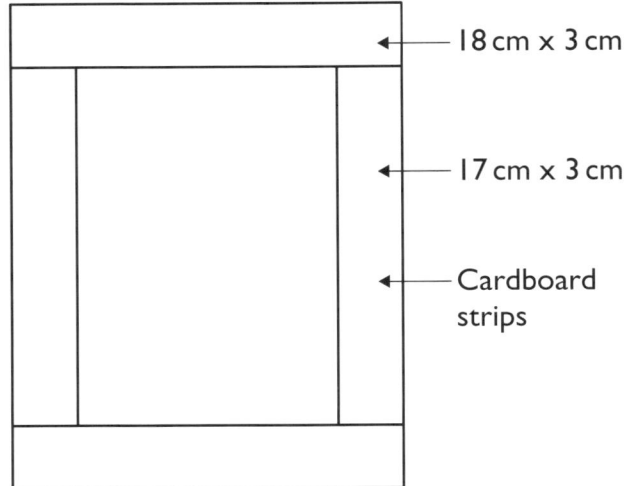

4. Cut out nine pieces of thin transparent plastic about 5.5 cm long and 3.5 cm wide. These represent small pieces of glass.

Figure 2

5. Make long strips of Plasticine and use them to stick a piece of plastic into the window frame as figure 2 shows. The Plasticine represents lead.

Plastic

Plasticine

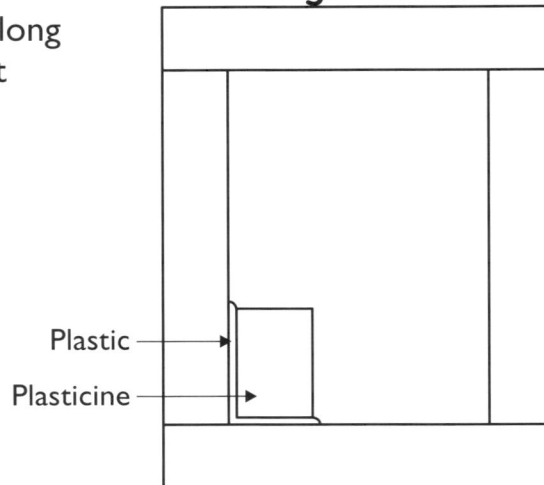

6. Begin adding other pieces of 'glass' to the 'window frame' with the 'lead' as figure 3 shows.

Figure 3

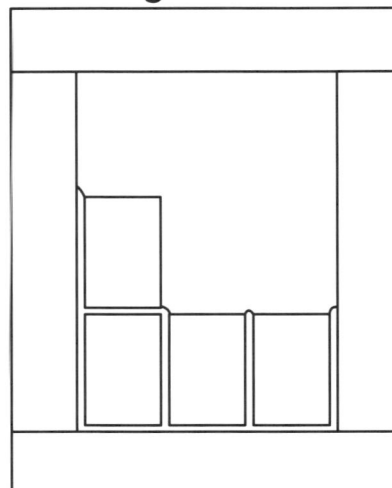

8. Add the other pieces to the window to complete it.

68

Make a leaded window

Age range
- Years 3/4 (SP4/5).
- Years 5/6 (SP6/7).

Resources
Each group will need some corrugated cardboard, some thin transparent plastic such as the transparent box used to package drinking straws, scissors, Plasticine, sticky tape. Secondary sources about Tudor windows (optional).

Using the worksheet
Glass was expensive in Tudor times and was made in small pieces. They were stuck together using lead to make large windows seen in large houses and churches. They were also used in smaller houses. As windows were expensive some Tudor families took their windows with them when they changed homes. You may like to tell the children they are going to make a window that can be moved around.

Younger students
Some of the students may need help in measuring out the window frames and the transparent plastic. When all the windows are finished, they could be stuck to the classroom window so the students can gain a little knowledge of what a large Tudor window was like.

Outcomes
The students:
- Know about the structure of Tudor windows.
- Can make measurements.
- Can follow instructions and work safely.

Older students
The students should be able to work through the activity with little assistance. They may like to compare their windows with photographs of windows in Tudor buildings.

Outcomes
The students:
- Know about the structure of Tudor windows.
- Can make a model of a window and assess its authenticity.

Can you dance?

A. Before you start note the time.

B. Take a partner and try this dance. The boy should escort the girl to the dance floor holding her right hand with his left hand.

   1. Face your partner, bow and curtsey.

   2. Turn to the right and hold your partner's hand (boy's left hand, girl's right hand).

   3. Take six steps forwards.

   4. Release hands. Boy turns around by turning to his right. Girl turns round by turning to her left.

   5. Hold hands again (boy's right hand, girl's left hand).

   6. Take six steps back.

   7. Release hands again. Boy turns around by turning to his left. Girl turns round by turning to her right.

   8. Hold hands (boy's left hand, girl's right hand).

   9. Skip six times.

   10. Face your partner, bow and curtsey.

   11. Repeat steps 1 to 10.

C. When you have learned this dance. Note the time.

D. 1. How long did it take you to learn the dance? ✎ ....

   2. What do you think was the most difficult part to remember?

   ✎ ....

   3. Try and write some more steps to the dance.

   ✎ ....

   ✎ ....

   ✎ ....

Can you dance?

Age range
- Years 3/4 (SP4/5).
- Years 5/6 (SP6/7).

Resources
Copies of the worksheets.

Using the worksheet
The Tudors loved music and liked to dance. Here is a fictitious dance but it has elements of Tudor dances in it. You may like to use a tape or CD of Tudor dance music to accompany the dance. Select music that is slow. Later, you may select a faster piece of music. The emphasis here is on learning to dance. Some students will find this easier than others.

Younger students
You may like to arrange the students into pairs and get them up on a dance floor and go through the instructions on the sheet. Let them rehearse the dance a few times then try it on their own. You may have to help some students invent extra steps to the dance.

Outcomes
The students:
- Know that Tudors liked to dance.
- Can learn a simple dance.

Older students
The students can work in pairs to learn the dance, then perform it in groups of five or six pairs. The students may be able to work out an extra dance routine on their own but it should be in the style of the original dance and not involve rapid jumping or wildly waving arms.

Outcomes
The students:
- Know that Tudors liked to dance.
- Can learn a simple dance.

Make a maze

1. How long does it take you to find your way from A to B in this maze?

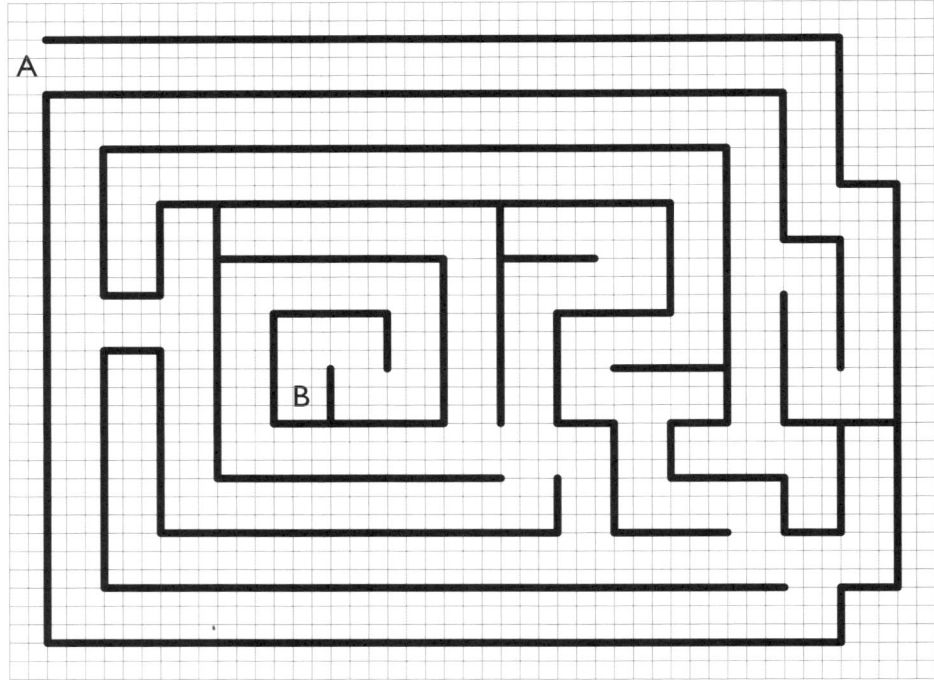

2. Once you have found the way try it again. How long does it take a second time.

3. Make your own maze. Ask a friend to try this maze and the one you have made. Which one do they find quicker to do?

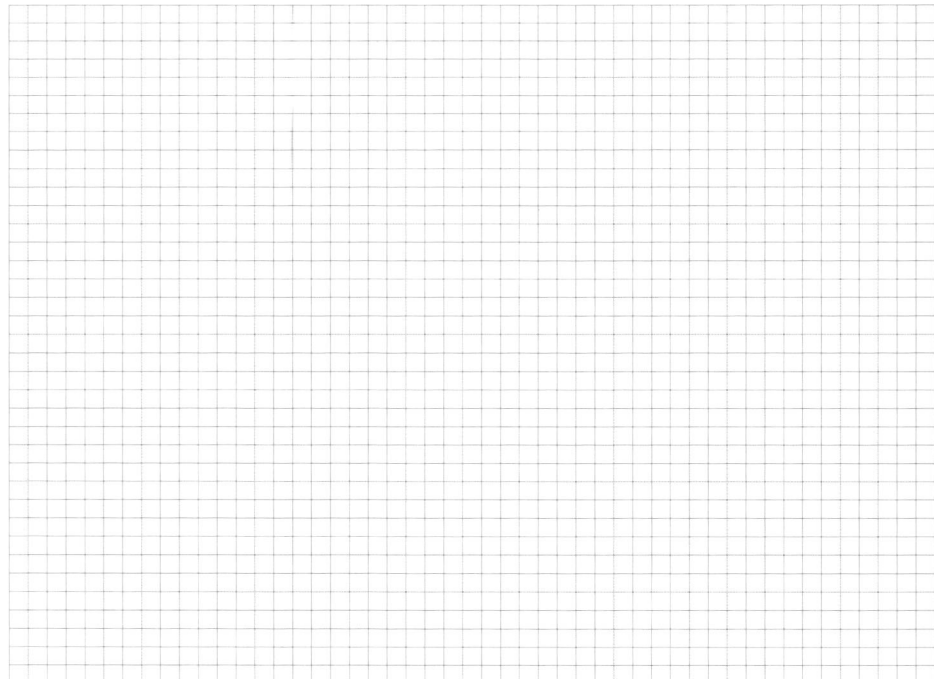

Make a maze

Age range
- Years 3/4 (SP4/5).
- Years 5/6 (SP6/7).

Resources
A photocopy of this sheet, graph paper,
pencil, clock.

Using the worksheet
Large Tudor houses also had large gardens. One
feature of the gardens was a maze. This was made
of thick evergreen bushes so it could be used at any
time of year. The dense foliage prevented people
seeing through the "walls" to help them find their
way. This is a plan of a simple maze.

Younger students
Let the students work through the questions on the
sheet. They may find graph paper easier to use for
drawing their plans than ordinary white paper.

Outcomes
The students:
- Know that a maze was a feature of a large
  Tudor garden.
- Can find their way through a maze.
- Can make a maze.

Older students
The students can work through the worksheet
on their own. They may like more and more
complicated mazes to try and defeat their friends.

Outcomes
The students:
- Know that a maze was a feature of a large
  Tudor garden.
- Can find their way through a maze.
- Can make a maze.

Spread ⑩ (pages 22–23)

The church loses its wealth

The purpose of the spread

Here we touch on the reformation from the point of view of how it affected the people in general.

Background

The period of Henry VIII and his six wives is, of course, one of the most turbulent in the whole of English history. It is covered in detail elsewhere, and here it is introduced in the context of the social changes that it brought about to the country as a whole.

The main point developed here is that, as a result of this shift of ownership, much land was redistributed (at a profit), and many merchants were able to buy into the landed class. At the same time the church lost much of its power and land.

The considerable effect this had on the religious buildings was amplified not just by Henry, but by his son Edward, who was an even more ardent Protestant.

Eventually many large abbeys and monasteries were destroyed, leaving the many ruins we find scattered around the country.

It might be worth considering the implications of this great change with students and how they might feel as the great religious and political upheavals went past.

Abbeys are quiet places today with their well kept lawns between ruined walls and arches. It is difficult to believe that they were once very busy places as the accompanying activity shows. Within the abbey there were monks with particular tasks. Here are just a few you may have met if you were travelling through Tudor England and called in at a monastery for a night's rest.

The guest house master. He welcomed guests and made them comfortable. He made sure that the floors were strewn with fragrant herbs and at night the fires were stoked with wood that burned with a pleasant smell (like silver birch) to help the guests sleep.

The fraterer looked after the dining room and made sure that all tables, seats and crockery were clean and ready for a meal. He would also make sure the room was free from cobwebs.

The kitchener was responsible for making sure that everyone in the abbey had a regular supply of food. To this end he kept checks on stores of food, availability of herbs in the herb garden, the quantity of fish in the abbey's ponds and number of rabbits in the warrens around the abbey.

The larderer was like a present day butcher. He killed and skinned livestock and prepared the meat for the spit or the pan. He was responsible for all the stored food.

When the abbeys were destroyed the monks lost their jobs. Many became teachers.

Daily life in a abbey

Here are the times for activities in an abbey over a period of twenty four hours. They are not in order.

12.30 p.m.	Work
Midnight	Matins
11.00 a.m.	Dinner
6.30 p.m.	Walking
8.00 a.m.	Terce
6.00 a.m.	Prime
7.30 p.m.	Bed time
9.00 a.m.	Meeting
10.50 a.m.	Hand washing
9.30 a.m.	Conversation
6.00 p.m.	Evening meal
10.00 a.m.	High mass
11.30 a.m.	Rest
1.00 a.m.	Lauds
7.00 a.m.	Reading
5.00 p.m.	Vespers
6.30 a.m.	Breakfast

Here are most of the places where one or more of the activities take place:

Dormitory   church   chapterhouse   cloister   lavatory   refectory

There are two activities which can take place in a variety of places which are they?

✎ ....   ✎ ....

Make a table with the headings 'Time', 'Activity', 'Place' and arrange the activities into chronological order starting at midnight. Then fill in the places where the activities occur.

Daily life in an abbey

Age range
- Years 3/4 (SP4/5).
- Years 5/6 (SP6/7).

Resources
The worksheet. Secondary sources about monastic life (optional).

Using the worksheet
The worksheet could be introduced after reading about the abbey on page 16 in 'Our town in 1500' or it can be introduced with this spread. The worksheet provides an opportunity to assess skills in constructing a timeline as well as giving a brief insight into monastic life. Matins, Terce, Prime, High Mass, Lauds and Vespers are all acts of worship in the church.

Younger students
The students could begin by working out a timeline for themselves on a school day. When they have finished the activity on the worksheet, they could compare their own timeline with that of the monks. The places where the activities take place are Matins – church, Lauds – church, Prime – church, Breakfast – refectory, Reading – cloister, Terce – church, Meeting – chapterhouse, Conversation – cloister, High mass – church, Hand washing – lavatory, Dinner – refectory, Rest – various places, Work – various places, Vespers – church, Evening meal – refectory, Walking – cloister, bed time – dormitory. You may point out that the monks return to the dormitory after Lauds.

Outcomes
The students can:
- Construct a timeline.
- Compare two timelines.

Older students
The answers for completing the table are given in the section for younger students. You may add that during meals the diners are not allowed to speak and readings on religious topics are made. The meeting deals with organisation of the abbey which may deal with giving out work to punishing monks who do not follow the rules. Work can vary from working on copying books to tending the fields, dealing with livestock or working in the herb garden.

The students could use this information together with the work in the table they have constructed to write an imaginary account of living in an abbey.

Outcomes
The students can:
- Construct a timeline.
- Use information and imagination to write creatively.

Make a monastery herb garden

Here is information about some of the plants that were grown in a monastery garden. If you follow the instructions for care you may be able to turn part of your school grounds into a monastery herb garden.

Garlic

Split up a bulb into its segments. They are called cloves. Plant the cloves in the ground with the pointed end uppermost. It likes a sunny position and moist, well drained soil. Garlic can be planted in March and October.

The crushed cloves were mixed with goose grease to make an ointment to rub on the body to ease chest diseases.

Marjoram

Sow marjoram seeds in March or April in pots. Keep the pots inside on a sunny windowsill. Marjoram can be grown indoors on a sunny windowsill or it can be planted out in the ground during the summer. It does not like very cold weather and may not survive the winter outside.

Marjoram was used to ease rheumatic complaints and as its leaves give off a pleasant smell when they are crushed it was strewn on stone floors so that the smell was released when people walked on it.

Mint

Mint is usually grown from its roots. The roots can be planted out in spring or autumn. They are best kept in a container as they can spread all over a garden. They can also be grown indoors.

Mint was used to give flavour to food and to ease digestive disorders.

Rosemary

Rosemary seeds can be sown in April and May. New plants can also be made from old ones by taking cuttings. A fifteen centimetre long branch of a Rosemary bush is cut off and the cut end is planted in seed compost mixed with a little sand. Rosemary likes a well drained soil in a sunny position sheltered from the wind. It can also be grown indoors.

Rosemary was scattered on stone floors so that its pleasant smell was released when people walked on it. It was sometimes used instead of incense in religious services.

78

Make a monastery herb garden

Age range
- Years 3/4 (SP4/5).
- Years 5/6 (SP6/7).

Resources
A photocopy of the sheet. Garlic bulbs, trowel, marjoram seeds (or you can buy plants), pots, seed compost, mint (probably given away by someone who has too much in their garden), containers, Rosemary seeds or plants, containers, knife for cuttings (adult use only) seed compost, sand, pots, Sage plants, southernwood and thyme (optional extras).

Using the worksheet
You may like to introduce this worksheet after the last one using the period of work in the timeline as a link. Monasteries had herb gardens to provide plants for improving the taste of food, the smell of the air in the buildings, easing ailments and even getting rid of fleas! The worksheet may be simply used to provide a comprehension exercise or it may be used as a basis for a class project to set up a herb garden. With this latter role in mind here are details of three more herbs that can be easily added to the ones on the worksheet.

Sage can be bought as a small plant and allowed to grow. The monks had many medicinal uses for it from aiding the digestive process to curing snakebites! If grown indoors it is claimed it keeps insects away.

Southernwood can be bought as a small plant and will grow to over a metre in height. It has a sweet smell and was used to rid clothes of fleas.

Thyme seeds can be sown in April or May. The plants can be grown in the ground or in pots. Thyme was used to attract bees to gardens so plants could be pollinated and fruits grown. It was also used as a strewing plant like rosemary and marjoram.

If taking cuttings make sure you follow your school policies on safety.

Younger students
You could provide the students with the extra information about the three other plants and then ask them to make a table of the uses of the plants in monasteries. You could ask the students to work in groups to design a herb garden for the school and let them compare their ideas.

Outcomes
The students:
- Know about the uses of herbs in a monastery.
- Can use information to help them plan a project.

Older students
The students could be challenged to set up a herb garden and to devise a timeline based on the present time for the next twelve months. A timetable could be planned and the students could work together to see if their ideas can be achieved. The students can be reminded that the monks worked together to achieve the aims of the abbey and these included growing plants and caring for the needy.

Outcomes
The students can:
- Use information to plan a project.
- Devise a schedule based on information.
- Work cooperatively to achieve an aim.

Chapter 3: The times of Queen Elizabeth I and after

Spread ⑪ (pages 24–25)

Francis Drake and the Armada

The purpose of the spread

This spread is concerned with one of the great battles of the Tudor times.

Background

This is, of course, one of the most famous and important battles in English history. It is included in this book as an example of how England was still very much connected with the rest of Europe and her growing power and influence.

Although the attempted invasion occurred in Elizabeth's reign, the cause for it dated back to her father and his break from Rome. For the time that Mary was on the throne, it was hoped that things would return to normal, but when Elizabeth became monarch it was clear that the cause of catholicism was not going to be served in the future.

There were several factors that could be discussed with students. The first concerns the historic causes for the decision to invade. Another is the technology that was used. Many people have, in the past, imagined small English ships setting out to defeat large Spanish galleons in a sort of David and Goliath battle. However, research has shown that this was nothing of the sort.

The English had become more of a maritime power, and as such had invested in technology of boat design as well as gun design. The English men of war were both more modern in design and larger than their Spanish counterparts. The Spanish would therefore not want to engage in battle if they could possibly avoid it.

The weaponry on the Spanish ships was unsuited to running battles. The guns were too long and heavy for the ships and could not easily be reloaded. This meant they were greatly disadvantaged compared with the English cannon, which could be reloaded in a fraction of the time. The Spanish were also distant from places where they could restock, whereas the English could restock in local ports.

But all ships of the time were at the mercy of the weather to a large degree and so manoeuvrability was limited. But when they were at anchor, the Spanish ships became much more vulnerable because they were potential targets for fireships – when the wind direction was right. By anchoring close together in a defensive position they were particularly liable to destruction by fireships.

The strategy of the English was thus to harass the enemy until a moment came when they were at a disadvantage. That moment came off Calais.

The importance of the defeat of the Armada was profound, in securing the independence of England and giving confidence that she could develop into a more powerful country.

Fireships and hellburners

Sailors had known about fireships for a long time and they had been widely used in battles in the past. In 1585 a new kind of fireship was used in a battle. It was called a hellburner and was invented by the Italian engineer called Federigo Giambelli. They are thought to have been loaded with gunpowder and metal bars so that when a ship was ablaze it blew up and scattered hot iron over a wide area causing a large amount of damage.

At the time when the Armada sailed towards England, the Spanish knew that Giambelli was in London. He was working on a floating barrier across the Thames to keep the Armada out.

After a battle with the English fleet, the Armada anchored off the coast of France at Calais to pick up more troops for a full scale invasion of England. The English commanders realised that they had not much time to act and knew that while the Armada was anchored they could be attacked by fireships. Some fireships were being prepared at Dover and one of the commanders was sent in a small boat to collect them. However, the other commanders decided that these fireships may not reach them in time so the captains of eight ships volunteered their crafts to be made into fireships. The ships were larger than normal fireships but they were packed with firewood from the kitchens of other ships, spare timbers for repairing damaged ships and ropes and lamp oil.

The Spaniards had prepared to deal with fireships by having small boats called pinnaces ready to pull them out of the way. However when they saw the size of the ships, they thought of Giambelli and his hellburners and decided to cut their anchors quickly and get the battleships out of the way.

The Spanish ships scattered along the coast and the English ships chased after them using their superior guns to damage them so they could not fight. The Commanders of the Armada decided to escape by sailing around Great Britain but many ships were lost on the way home.

1. Why was a hellburner more frightening than a fireship?

   ✎ ....

2. What might the Spanish have thought Giambelli was doing in England?

   ✎ ....

3. How were the fireships used by the English different from other fireships?

   ✎ ....

4. When the Spanish saw the English fireships why might they have thought they were hellburners?

   ✎ ....

5. Imagine you are commanding the crew of a pinnace. (i) How would you feel when you saw that the fireships were larger than expected? (ii) Would you think it was worth trying to get them out of the way of the Armada? Explain your answer.

   ✎ ....

82

Fireships and hellburners

Age range
- Years 3/4 (SP4/5).
- Years 5/6 (SP6/7).

Resources
A photocopy of the sheet.

Using the worksheet
You could begin by saying that when events are studied in history sometimes things are not just as straightforward as they seem. The use of fireships on the Armada is an example. Fireships had been used in the past and the Spanish expected the English to use them if they got the chance. However, they had made precautions by having small boats called pinnaces patrolling the Armada at anchor so that fireships could be pulled out of the way. You do not need to go further in the introduction but the purpose of the activity is to show the students that the Spaniards knowledge of the inventor of the hellburners being in London and the appearance of larger fireships than usual caused the Spanish to believe they were being attacked by hellburners so decided to get away.

Younger students
The students may need help in making the connections between Giambelli and the decision not to wait for the real fireships to arrive.
1) It could cause much greater damage.
2) Building hellburners.
3) They were larger than other fireships.
4) Their larger size and the knowledge that Giambelli was in London.
5) (i) Surprised and frightened. (ii) Some may answer that it would be worth getting them out of the way but there is a good chance that they would explode before they were at a safe distance. Others may say that it was too dangerous to risk the crew when the ships could explode at any moment so the only thing to do was for the Armada to get away.

Outcomes
The students:
- Know that several factors can influence the course of events.
- Can use their imagination to describe what it might be like to meet a large fireship.

Older students
The students could read through the account and answer the questions. From the answers, you may assess which students have made the connections to account for why the Spaniards decided to "cut and run".

Outcomes
The students:
- Know that several factors can influence the course of events.
- Can use their imagination to see how people in the past made decisions.

Spread ⑫ (pages 26–27)

Our village in 1600

The purpose of the spread

This spread concentrates on the changes that took place in homes over the Elizabethan period.

Background

One of the most enduring tangible features of Tudor times are the black and white, or magpie, buildings. They are domestic buildings, homes for families of the moderately well off, not simply palaces of the very wealthy.

These are the first houses to survive to present times in large numbers.

Students need to be reminded that magpie houses are often a caricature of the times. Many other houses of this age were built that did not have the magpie characteristics, Where these are found is in areas where building stone was plentiful and wood scarce. So, buildings of similar date in the Pennines are mainly built of stone, for example.

But what is important, and characteristic of all houses of the middle classes is that there was enough money around to allow them to be rebuilt and repurposed, hence the name of the period as The Great Rebuilding.

As important as anything is the separation of functions. Where people had lived in long barns before, perhaps just one or two rooms, with family at one end, now they were building outhouses for their animals and special workshops for the things they did, such as smith's work or brewing.

As a result, the house became a place for living in. And with this came the idea of having more fashion conscious goods around the home. Goods become worth something as their quality was higher and they are mentioned in wills.

It is also interesting to students to understand why some Tudor buildings have low roofs and why you step down into some buildings. Were the Tudors much shorter than us? The answer is that they were shorter than us, but the reason for the low ceilings and sometimes lowered floors is that not everyone could afford to rebuild and so some simply put in an extra floor within the existing house. This resulted in the downstairs floor having a low ceiling.

How walls change

Figure 1

cardboard with lines drawn on

lollipop sticks

1. Cut out two pieces of cardboard about 3.5 cm wide and 7 cm long.

2. Draw lines on the pieces of cardboard to represent the outline of stones and then stick them to three lolly sticks as shown in figure 1. The lolly sticks represent timbers in a timber framed house.

Figure 2

matchsticks stuck over top

3. Glue matchsticks to the lolly sticks as shown in figure 2. They represent laths used at a later date to cover the stonework and provide a base for plaster.

Figure 3

Plasticine on top

4. Cover the matchsticks with Plasticine as shown in figure 3. This represents plaster.

Figure 4

card squares with border drawn on to represent wooden panels

5. Cut out some pieces of card 4 cm square. Draw a border on each one. Each card represents a wooden panel. Stick the cards on the "plaster" to make a "wooden panelled" wall as shown in figure 4.

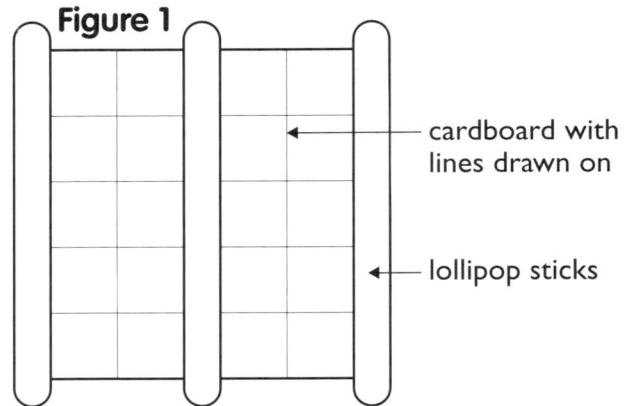

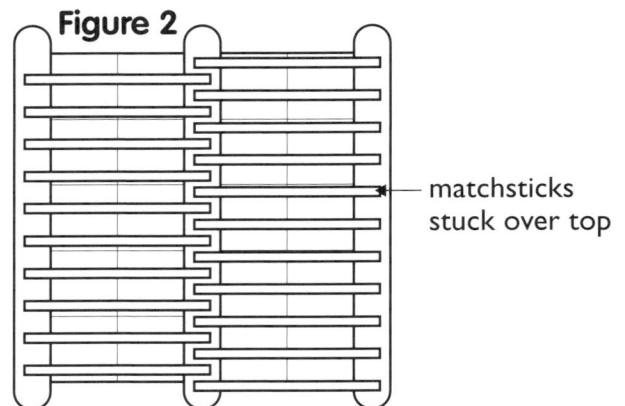

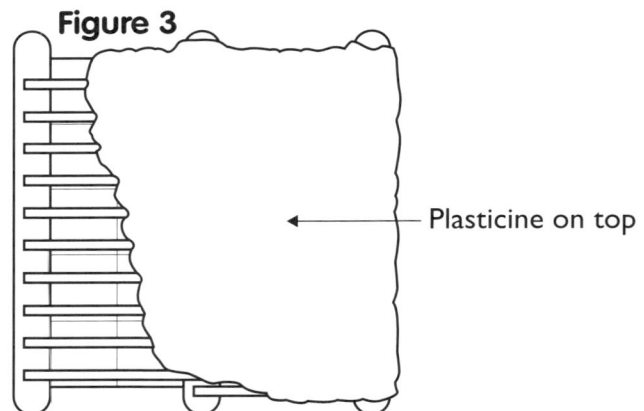

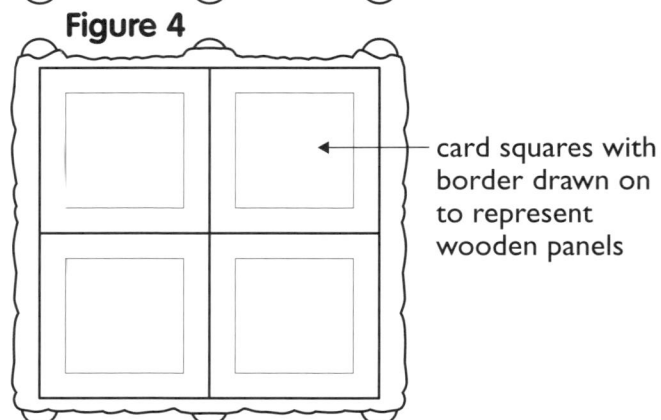

How walls change

Age range
- Years 3/4 (SP4/5).
- Years 5/6 (SP6/7).

Resources
Each group will need three lolly sticks, a piece of corrugated cardboard, about thirty matches (with no heads on), a ball of Plasticine, ruler, pen. Secondary sources about secret doors and passages (optional for older students).

Using the worksheet
We usually think of archaeology to do with digging in the ground but it can also involve the study of walls and digging into them to find out how a building has changed over time. In this model, a timber framed wall has stones between the timbers. At a later date laths were added to the timber frames on the inside of the building. In a real wall the laths would be nailed end to end on the timbers but in this model they are placed one end above another end simply because the lolly stick is not wide enough for them to be joined end to end. The laths were then covered in plaster and at an even later date, perhaps in Victorian times, the plaster was covered over by wood panelling. Some students may build the walls and others, who have been working on another activity and not seen their construction, could behave like archaeologists and remove the layers of the wall and report on its structure.

Younger students
The students can work through the steps on their own. When they apply the Plasticine it should only be a thin layer. They should be careful as they smear it on not to dislodge any of the laths.

Outcomes
The students:
- Know that an old wall may have many layers on the inside.
- Can make a model of an old wall or remove layers and report on the wall's structure.

Older students
When the students have completed their task they could use secondary sources to find out about panels in walls that reveal secret cupboards or secret doors leading to passages or priest holes.

Outcomes
The students:
- Know that an old wall may have many layers on the inside.
- Can make a model of an old wall or remove layers and report on the wall's structure.

Spread ⓯ (pages 28–29)

Our town in 1600

The purpose of the spread

Here we provide the contrast in building design and other features with those near the beginning of Tudor times. Using this we can see how rich and poor have fared.

Background

When students look at the town in 1600 and compare it with 1500 they should immediately notice a difference in the density of the buildings. Towns are growing, and they have grown mainly by infilling. At the same time, buildings have become multistorey with workshops below and living quarters above.

Why is it that the towns have infilled in this way? Much of it is to do with the nature of transport. People moved on foot or pushed handcarts. As a result, it was vital that the distance travelled was as small as possible so that time would not be wasted in moving between locations. The great growth of the size of towns and cities that we see today is, of course, a result of the development of mass transport beginning in the middle of the 19th century. It did not occur at this time.

People who owned land in the town could also make a good profit by building on their land and renting out the buildings.

As people owned plots which were large and often reached down to the river, they were anxious to make the best use of the plot possible. So courts developed behind the main street frontage, reached by narrow side alleys. This meant that an owner might be able to get dozens of houses on what had once been his market garden. The profit realised was substantial even if the quality of the rented accommodation was mostly poor.

This time thus sees the development of intricate street patterns with alleys and courts in what in 1500 had been a relatively uncrowded town and perhaps no more than a single street.

There is still no sewage system or clean water and so the filth and squalor of the town is growing. The health of its residents is also poor and with so many people close together, the spread of infectious diseases readily occurs.

There are now no places to grow food in the town and so it must all be brought in and bought in markets. The town has become entirely dependent on the countryside. There is no refrigeration and so animals are still walked into the town and then slaughtered, so some activities are placed where possible on the town outskirts so as to keep the smell from the centre.

Much of the 1600 town has now been cleared away, often in Victorian times when bigger roads were needed for vehicular traffic. But side alleys often still give much of a flavour of what it was like.

A day in the life of a town

Midnight   All are asleep.

3.00 a.m.   Milkmaids get up.

4.00 a.m.   Servants are having breakfast.

5.00 a.m.   The church bell rings. Some people go to the early morning service.

6.00 a.m.   The shops open.

7.00 a.m.   Everyone is at work or at school.

8.00 a.m.   Breakfast time.

9.00 a.m.   People buying and selling in the market place.

11.00 a.m.   Everyone stops work to have a meal.

5.00 p.m.   School finishes for the day.
                  Rich people have supper.

7.00 p.m.   The shops close.
                  Poorer working people have their suppers when they get home.

1. How long are children at school?

    ✎ ....

2. How long are the shops open?

    ✎ ....

3. On a separate sheet of paper, construct a timeline for a day in the life of your town.

4. How does your timeline compare with this one?

    ✎ ....

A day in the life of a town

Age range
- Years 3/4 (SP4/5).
- Years 5/6 (SP6/7).

Resources
A photocopy of the sheet. Secondary sources about night-time in Tudor towns (optional for older students).

Using the worksheet
If you have done activity **10A** 'Daily life in an abbey' you may like to remind the students of it then move on to consider how people in towns lived.

Younger students
The students could work through the questions. They may need help with finding times when shops open and close and may need to be reminded about supermarkets which are open all night. This activity can be linked with activities **19A**, **19B** and **19C** which deals with school work.

Answers
1. Ten hours.
2. 13 hours.

Outcomes
The students can:
- Extract information from a timeline.
- Make and compare timelines.

Older students
The students could work through the questions. They may like to consider people who work through the night in today's towns and look for people who work through the night in Tudor times. They may find that a bell man moved round the town shouting out the hours and that night watchmen or soldiers were employed to keep a look out for thieves.

Outcomes
The students can:
- Extract information from a timeline.
- Make and compare timelines.

Make a house

1. You are going to make a model house out of three milk cartons, six lolly sticks and pieces of paper and card. They are to be assembled as figure 1 shows.

2. Before you assemble the cartons, cover the sides which are to be seen with white paper.

3. Draw a pattern of the timbers. There were three basic styles as figure 2 shows. Select one style for your house and draw it in with a black pen. Look at photographs of houses in your book to see how doors and windows fitted in and draw them on the wall of your house.

4. Stick the lolly sticks to the top of the lower carton and then stick the other cartons on top. Make sure the two upper cartons stick closely together.

5. Cut out two pieces of card 12 cm by 7 cm for the roof. Cut out two triangular pieces of card with a base of 11 cm and a height of 5 cm for the gable ends of the house. Make your timber pattern on the gable ends.

6. Bend some smaller pieces of card to make connectors between the roof pieces and the gable ends as figure 3 shows.

7. Rest the roof on top of the two cartons. You may have to move the gables in a little as shown in figure 4 to make the roof sit comfortably on top of the cartons.

Figure 1

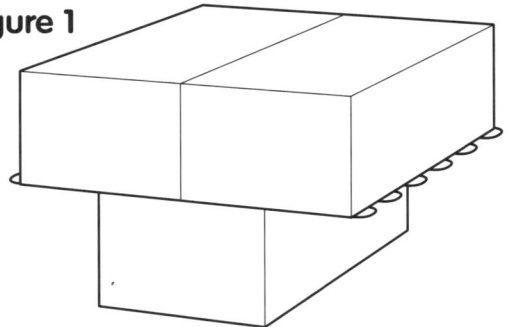

Figure 2

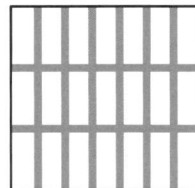

Northern England

Eastern England

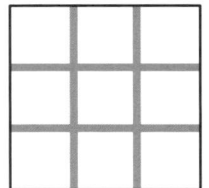

Western England and Wales

Figure 3

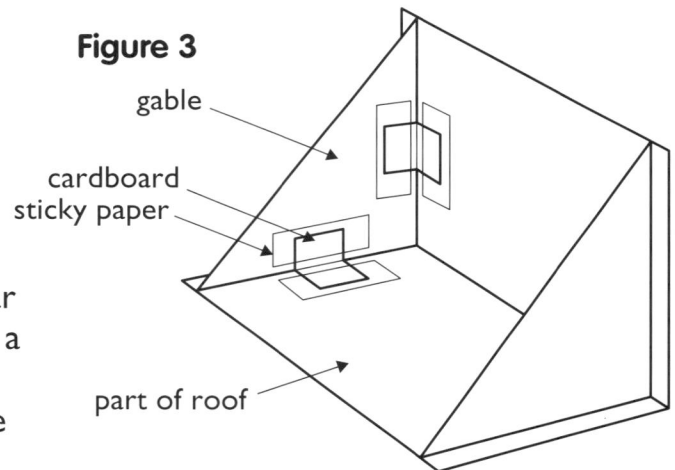

gable

cardboard
sticky paper

part of roof

Figure 4

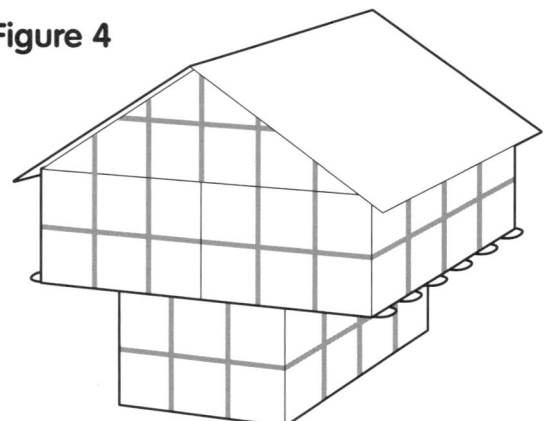

Make a house

Age range
- Years 3/4 (SP4/5).
- Years 5/6 (SP6/7).

Resources
Three milk cartons, six lolly sticks, paper, scissors, card, sticky paper, glue.

Using the worksheet
When Tudor families became more affluent, they needed larger houses. The plots of land on which they stood did not have space for extensions on the ground so the upper floors were extended by overhangs called jetties. These created extra floor space in the upper storeys to cope with the owner's demand. They also provided a cantilever structure which helped distribute the extra weight carried by the floors and prevented the houses collapsing. A simple illustration of the use of jetties can be given by using milk cartons from the infant department They are covered in paper and decorated in an appropriate timber style then assembled to make a house. If several groups in the class try this activity they can make a narrow street with overhangs as seen in some of the pictures in the student book. The dimensions of the roof are given to match cartons which are about 11 cm x 5 cm x 4 cm. As an extension you could ask the students to design and make a chimney for the house.

Younger students
The children need to measure the dimensions of the sides they are to cover with paper. They then measure out the dimensions on white paper and cut it out. These are then stuck on the cartons. The students may need help with assembling the roof.

Outcomes
The students:
- Know how Tudors created extra space in their houses.
- Can follow instructions to make a model house.

Older students
The students may make measurements of the paper, as explained for younger students, or simply put the carton sides on the paper and draw round them, then cut out the paper "walls". Ambitious students could try making the pattern with matchsticks (with heads removed) and glue but they will need patience and must take great care as it is rather difficult.

Outcomes
The students:
- Know how Tudors created extra space in their houses.
- Can follow instructions to make a model house.

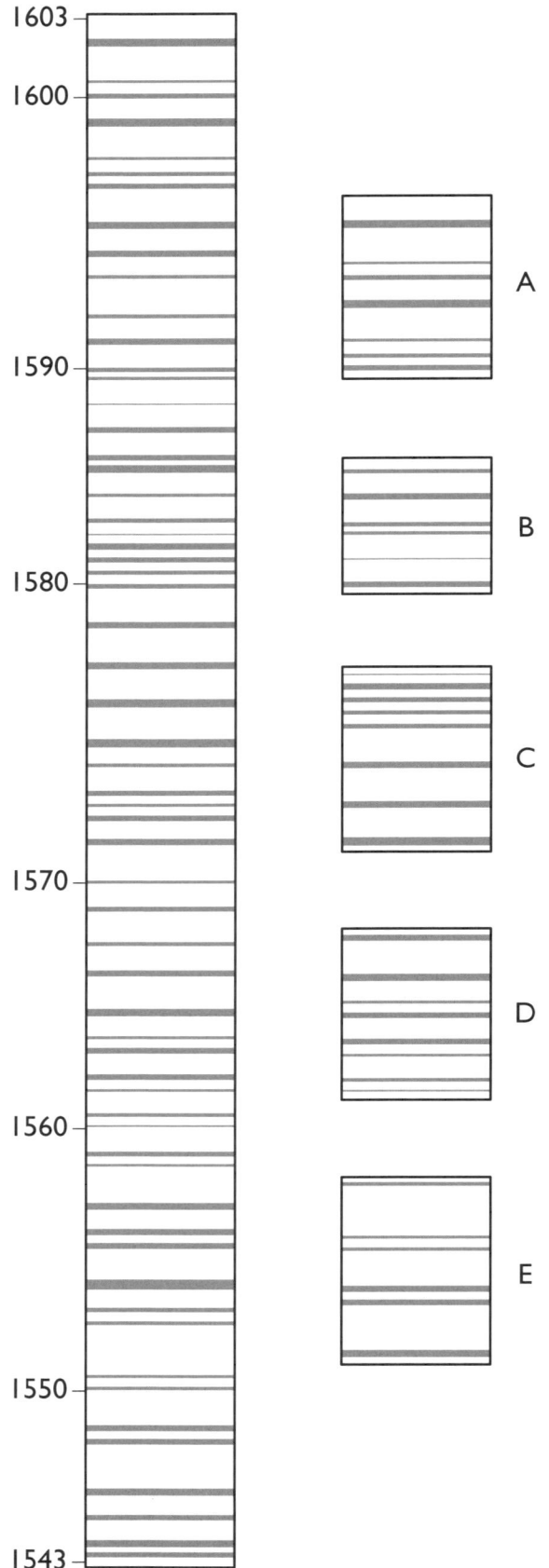

Dating wood with tree rings

The left-hand column represents wood showing tree rings from 1603 back to 1543.

A to E represent pieces of wood found in the timber frames of five houses in a town.

Cut out A to E and match the tree rings in each piece to the column to find the time when each piece of wood was growing.

Write your answers below.

A ✎ ....

B ✎ ....

C ✎ ....

D ✎ ....

E ✎ ....

Dating wood with tree rings

Age range
- Years 3/4 (SP4/5).
- Years 5/6 (SP6/7).

Resources
A photocopy of the sheet.

Using the worksheet
You may like to begin by asking the class how the age of a tree can be worked out. Some may say that when a tree is cut down the rings in the stump can be counted. Build on this to say that many trees produce a ring of growth for each year of their life. When conditions are good the ring is broad and when they are bad the ring is narrow. As all trees producing rings behave in this way, it is possible to compare the rings of an old tree with a young tree and see that the rings of the young tree match the latter stages of life in the older tree. By seeing how patterns overlap in this way a long column of tree ring patterns passing back many centuries can be worked out. In this activity a fictitious pattern for most of the Tudor period is shown to help the students appreciate how archaeologists carry out tree ring dating. Its technical name is dendrochronology.

Younger students
Let the students work through the sheet. When they have finished ask them to write down the names of the timbers in order of age starting with the youngest. Ask them to find out which timbers had grown in Queen Elizabeth's reign.

Answers (See also diagram opposite)
A. Late 1590s to early 1600s.
B. Late 1580s to early 1590s.
C. Late 1570s to early 1580s.
D. 1560s.
E. Late 1540s to early 1550s.

Outcomes
The students can:
- Match patterns of tree rings.
- Understand how timbers can be dated using their tree rings.

Older students
Let the students work through the sheet. When they have finished ask them to write down the names of the timbers in order of age starting with the youngest. Ask the students the following questions:
1. Which monarchs were on the throne during the time covered by the column on the left? (Henry VIII, Edward VI, Mary I, Elizabeth I)
2. Which monarchs were on the throne when the five pieces of timber were growing? (A to D – Elizabeth I; E – Edward VI)
3. Which piece of timber was growing when the England defeated the Armada? (B)

Outcomes
The students can:
- Match patterns of tree rings.
- Understand how timbers can be dated using their tree rings.
- Relate tree ring growth to events in history.

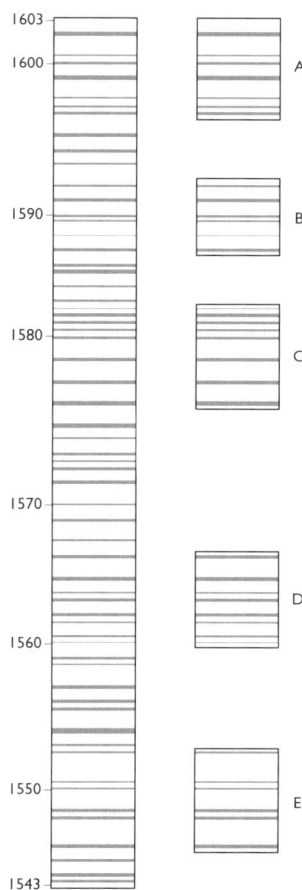

Spread **14** (pages 30–31)

Inside a Tudor town house

The purpose of the spread

This spread focuses in more detail on the internal structure of a town house.

Background

We need always to keep in mind that the town house was probably owned by the person who also rented out houses built behind. The idea of a town house has developed, with people building into continuous frontages.

At the same time, the upper floors of building began to be built so they overhung. More floor space could be gained this way. In side alleys the opposite buildings might be so close that people in one could shake hands with people in another. The close proximity of building all made from wood in an era of open hearths was, of course, a recipe for fire disaster as dramatically witnessed just over half a century later with the Great Fire of London. But London would not be unique. Disastrous fires were commonplace in most towns.

The town house was a place where people could show off their wealth. They could, for example, have glass in their windows. The windows could be much larger, which needed even more expensive glass. The house could have three floors instead of two.

What happened inside the house would depend on the status of the people who lived in it. In the case of the very wealthy, the ground level would be used to meet visitors, or it might be a hallway to a grand staircase that led to public rooms on the first floor. Servants would live in the basement or the attic.

If the house belonged to a merchant, then the ground floor would be a warehouse or workshop. The first floor would be where the owner lived and any upper floors used for renting out or for servants.

People would not have been used to the private space that we now expect and enjoy. Instead, it would have been perfectly common for each room of a house to be home to an entire family.

Notice that in this house there is no water or toilet. Water would have to come from a well. Toilet matters went into the street unless you were wealthy enough to have a closet that you paid to have emptied. If the well was shallow, then you might get bacteria from human waste into the water. This was a recipe for diseases such as cholera, although no one knew this at the time.

Make a board game called Merelles

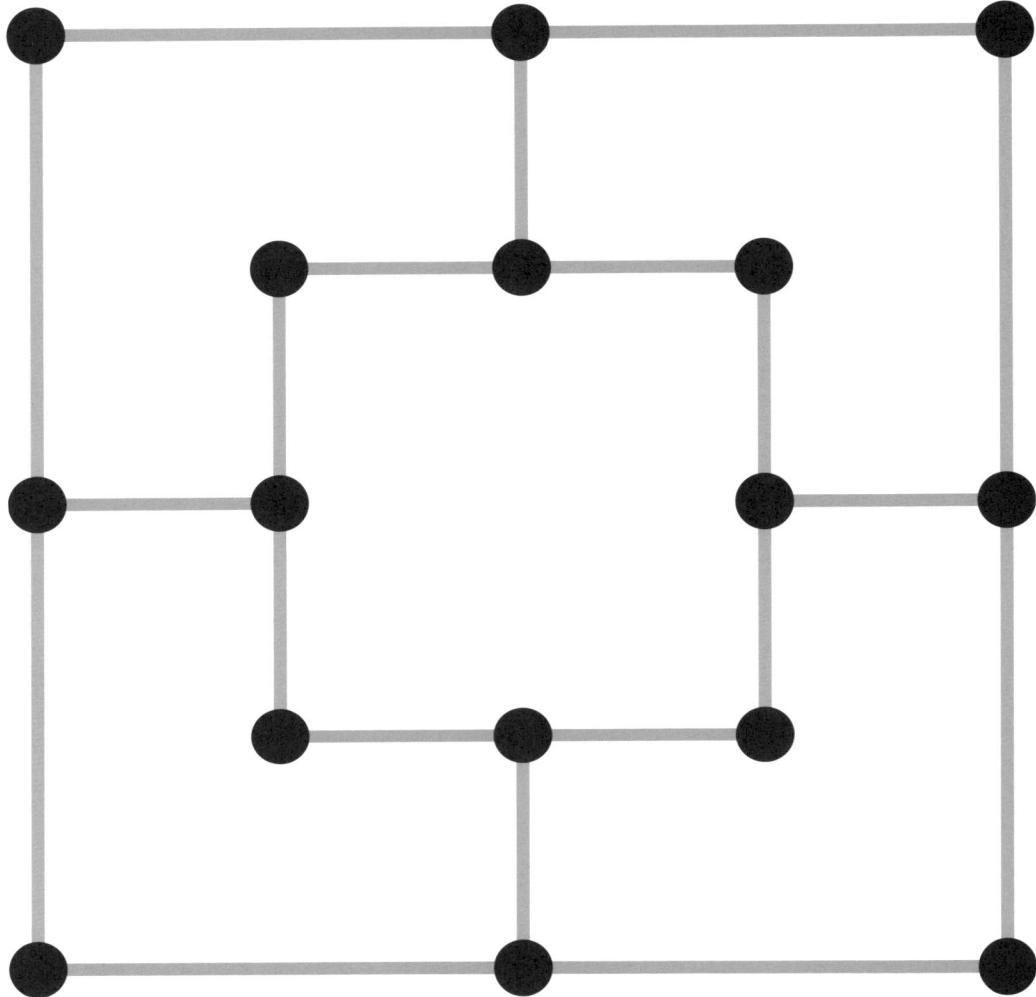

1. Make a copy of the lines and dots above onto a large piece of card.

2. Cut out some circular counters from another piece of card or use ten small coins.

3. Choose one person to play with.

4. Take turns at putting counters on the dots on the board. You should try and get three counters in a row before your opponent does.

5. If you get all the counters on the board without getting three in a row, you can start to move the counters in the following way. You can move a counter to a dot next to it which has not got a counter.

6. When someone gets three counters in a row they are the winner.

Make a board game called Merelles

Age range
- Years 3/4 (SP4/5).
- Years 5/6 (SP6/7).

Resources
A photocopy of the sheet. A large piece of card.
A smaller piece of card from which to cut counters,
scissors, coins.

Using the worksheet
The worksheet can be used to show the students a
pastime that was played inside. You may like to use
this activity as part of a Tudor day exercise to help
the students appreciate a little of Tudor life.

Younger students
The students can focus on making the game and
playing it.

Outcomes
The students can:
- Follow instructions to make and play a game
  from Tudor times.

Older students
When the students have made their games they
could organise a knock out championship.

Outcomes
The students can:
- Follow instructions to make and play a game
  from Tudor times.

Spread ⓯ (pages 32–33)

Furniture and fittings

The purpose of the spread

This spread concentrates on utensils and other fittings and compares them with modern versions.

Background

We have now brought students to a point where they have some experience of the later Tudor period and we introduce here the artefact of a will as a source of historical information.

The whole spread is based on the information from wills.

This gives an opportunity for students to look at some other wills from museums.

These are, of course, not the poorest people, but those with sufficient resources to think it useful to make a will. But most are not the wealthiest, either. So we get an opportunity to see the range of belongings that a person might have. This is a significant addition to the materials that are now available in museums because it tells us about the balance of items, and also points to items as being common that are not well preserved through to modern times, such as mattresses and clothing.

Using their wills and artefacts, we can piece together what it might have been like in a Tudor house more accurately than for previous periods. It is this kind of information that reconstructions are based on.

Students can also appreciate how some changes have occurred that are significant in the development of household equipment.

Much more furniture is now assembled for the use of people of modest means, something that would only have been available to the wealthy before.

Here are three more items that were found in Tudor homes:

The salt or salter. This container held as its name suggests the salt. Salt was regarded as the most important item in a meal and was accordingly housed in as grand a container as the householder could afford. It was placed near the top of the table where the head of the household and his guests dined. People of lesser worth in the household dined "below the salt".

The spice box. As trade increased with other parts of the world, spices became more readily available and were also considered important additions to a meal. They were stored in spice boxes. Queen Elizabeth I had one covered in jewels such as amethysts and rubies.

The pomander. This was a sphere of metal or wood with holes in it which contained pleasant smelling herbs and spices. It replaced the pomanders made from oranges, which towards the end of Tudor times, were considered to give too strong a smell.

What did he leave behind?

Thomas Smith died without making a will. An inventory or list was made of everything that he owned. Here is a section from the inventory:

	£	s	d
six silver spones	1	10	0
fower candlstiks		4	8
fower plates, fower dyces fower sawsers and one basene		8	6
five panes	1	12	0
six poetts	1	4	0
fower drinking cups			8
one gown		7	0
30 shepe	3	8	4
14 lames	1	0	8
Whool		18	6
Three peece of whoolen chlothe	6	6	0

1. What was each silver spoon valued at?

   ✎ ....

2. What was each candlestick valued at?

   ✎ ....

3. What was the total value of the items in the list?

   ✎ ....

4. What evidence suggests that Thomas Smith was a farmer?

   ✎ ....

5. Is there any evidence to suggest that Thomas Smith was involved with weaving? Explain your answer.

   ✎ ....

6. On a separate sheet, make an inventory of your pencil case or school bag. How much do you think the items are worth?

What did he leave behind?

Age range
- Years 3/4 (SP4/5).
- Years 5/6 (SP6/7).

Resources
A photocopy of the worksheet, a pencil case or school bag. Older students could use secondary sources featuring written materials that can be used as evidence.

Using the worksheet
If someone died without making a will in Tudor times, an inventory had to be made. Other people, such as family members, friends or people who were in the same business as the deceased, assessed the value of the possessions. When the assessment was complete a portion of the value of the goods had to be given to the poor. This activity allows the students to revisit work on money and spellings that were featured in activities **6B** and **6C**. You need to approach question 6 with sensitivity and where appropriate delete it by blanking out when you make your copies.

Younger students
The students may need help in performing the calculations and deciphering some of the words.

Answers
1. 5s 0d; 2. 1s 2d; 3. £17 0s 4d; 4. He had 30 sheep and 14 lambs; 5. Yes. He had wool and pieces of woollen cloth that someone in his family might have woven.
Words fower = four, dyces = dishes, sawsers = saucers, basene = basin

Outcomes
The students can:
- Make calculations on money used in Tudor times.
- Identify words written in the Tudor style.
- Interpret written evidence.

Older students
Let the students work through the sheet on their own and give assistance when they require it. They might like to look at other written materials which can be used as evidence.

Outcomes
The students can:
- Make calculations on money used in Tudor times.
- Identify words written in the Tudor style.
- Interpret written evidence.

Spread ⑯ (pages 34–35)

What the Tudors ate and drank

The purpose of the spread

To compare the meals of the rich and the poor.

Background

The diets of the rich and poor were easy to compare. The rich ate huge quantities of meat and very few vegetables. In fact they considered vegetables to be beggary baggage with means that vegetables were only fit to be eaten by the poor. By contrast the poor ate little else than vegetables and bread. If they had a stroke of good fortune they may eat a little meat occasionally.

For those who could afford to eat meat it was important to be mindful of flesh days and fish days. Flesh days were Sunday to Thursday. Fish days (when it was illegal to eat meat) were Fridays and Saturdays. Also the forty days before Easter were fish days. People had to eat fish for religious reasons but fish days were also enforced to provide a trade for England's fishing fleet and control the population from eating too much meat when it was in short supply in the winter.

The diet of Tudors who were neither rich nor poor could be summed up as comprising bread, beef and beer.

Bread

The common loaf of bread in Tudor times was the manchet. This was flat and round like a large white bread roll today. When a family was very poor, bread would be made from peas, beans, lentils and acorns. Even corn used for feeding horses would be used.

Beef

There was not enough food to keep all the livestock on a farm through the winter so many animals were killed in the autumn. There was no means of refrigeration so the salt was added to the meat to prevent decay. Even so some meat went bad but was still served up for a meal. Spices and mustard sauce were used to improve the taste of salted meat or bad meat.

In Tudor times a group of foods were known as "white meats". These were all dairy products such as butter and cheese. Eggs were also included in this group.

Beer

Drinking water was a dangerous thing to do in insanitary Tudor times. However if the water was boiled as in the making of beer it was safe to drink. Many people made their own beer at home. Very weak beer called small beer was given to children. There was no tea or coffee in Tudor times, the rich did not drink beer. They drank wine.

On the dining table

Food was served in bowls or on large plates called platters. Poor people used a square piece of wood with a hollow in it. It was called a trencher and used like a plate. Food was placed in the hollow. Richer people had a pewter dish instead of a trencher. Food was eaten with a knife and spoon. Forks only became available to the rich towards the end of the Tudor period.

Make some marchpane (marzipan)

Marchpane was a food substance made in Tudor times from ground almonds, sugar and rose water. Tudor cooks used to add food colourings to it and shape it into models of animals, flowers, fruits and even ships and castles!

Today a similar substance called marzipan is made from ground almonds, icing sugar and egg whites and used in cake decoration.

Make some marzipan by following this recipe:

1. Put two cups of ground almonds in a bowl.

2. Sift four cups of icing sugar onto the almonds.

3. Make a hollow in the centre of the mixture.

4. Take the whites of two eggs and lightly beat them.

5. Pour the beaten egg whites into the hollow in the bowl.

6. Stir the egg whites, almonds, and icing sugar to make a paste.

7. Knead the paste to make it smooth.

8. If the marzipan is a little dry, add a small amount of lemon juice.

Colouring marzipan

1. Take some marzipan and cut off a piece you want to use.

2. Select a coloured paste and place a small amount on the marzipan.

3. Knead the paste into the marzipan until the marzipan has taken up the colour evenly.

4. To make the colour darker add more paste and knead again.

5. To make the colour paler add more marzipan and knead again.

Try and make some marzipan models of your own.

Make some marchpane (marzipan)

Age range
- Years 3/4 (SP4/5).
- Years 5/6 (SP6/7).

Resources
For the recipe: 250 g (2 cups) ground almonds, 450 g (4 cups) sifted icing (confectioner's) sugar, 2 egg whites, large bowl, small bowl, egg whisk or fork, spoon. Alternatively, marzipan can be bought in some supermarkets and health food shops. It is also sold by suppliers of cake decorations. The type needed for colouring is called white marzipan. Food colouring pastes, knife, boards. Lemon juice.

Using the worksheet
This activity can be used as a homework or you may like to demonstrate it to the students or let the students help you. If high hygienic standards can be maintained the students could try the recipe for themselves. Worksurfaces and equipment need to be dust and grease free and very clean. Hands and fingernails need to be very clean or plastic gloves may also be used.

Younger students
The students will need help at home or in school.

Outcomes
The students can:
- Follow a recipe and make a food.
- Add colour correctly to marzipan.
- Make a marzipan model.

Older students
The students may be able to follow the instructions on the sheet on their own.

Outcomes
The students can:
- Follow a recipe and make a food.
- Add colour correctly to marzipan.
- Make a marzipan model.

A Tudor meal

Rich people had large meals with many different kinds of meat and a few vegetables. Poor people had whatever they could afford – sometimes just bread. Use the information below to help you make a Tudor meal. It should be a meal for someone who is neither rich nor poor.

Meat

You can have any meat you like. Suitable meats could be chicken legs, slices of cooked meats. If you plan to have your meal on a Friday there should be no meat, only fish.

Sauces

Mustard sauce.

Pottage

There are many kinds of pottage. One made from peas looks a little like mushy peas so perhaps you could have a small bowl of mushy peas.

Salads

The Tudors enjoyed salads and made them from lettuce, radish, cress, endive and cucumber.

Bread

Many Tudors ate a flat round, white loaf called a manchet. You could use a large white flat bread roll.

Cheese

The Tudors had two kinds of cheeses – green cheese which was like cottage cheese and hard cheese which is similar to the hard cheeses we have today.

Fruits

Strawberries, peaches and apricots.

Pies

The Tudors made many kinds of pies. An apple or blackberry pie could remind you of this.

Tea and coffee were not available to Tudors. Rich Tudors drank wine while the poor drank beer. You could pretend to be a rich Tudor and use red or white grape juice for wine.

A Tudor meal

Age range
- Years 3/4 (SP4/5).
- Years 5/6 (SP6/7).

Resources
A copy of the worksheet. The students can select their own food from the list. They could put the food in wooden bowls and use a wooden plate or small circular bread board for their meal. A pot or pewter goblet could be used for the drink. Only knives and spoons can be used. Forks only started to come into general use at the end of the Tudor period. Vegetarians can substitute Quorn products for meat.

Using the worksheet
You could use this activity after the students have studied pages 34 and 35 in the student book. You could tell them that rich Tudors ate large amounts of meat and few vegetables. Poorer people ate more bread and vegetables and may have been unable to afford meat. If the students have studied a balanced diet, you may like them to assess the two Tudor diets and say which is more balanced (the diet of the poor). The students could then take the sheet home and see if they could have a Tudor meal at home. Alternatively if you are planning a Tudor day you may wish to send a copy of the sheet home with your covering letter about Tudor clothes so that the parents or carers could prepare the meal for lunch.

Younger students
The students may need help in selecting items for a meal. Some may tend to select too many items. They may wish to include too many items and make a feast.

Outcomes
The students can:
- Plan a meal using items available to the Tudors.
- Plan a meal which is nutritionally balanced.

Older students
The students may wish to work in pairs or groups and prepare a feast – each student bringing a selection of foods. Care must be taken that there will not be any wastage.

Outcomes
The students can:
- Plan a meal using items available to the Tudors.
- Plan a Tudor feast.
- Plan a meal which is nutritionally balanced.

Spread ⑰ (pages 36–37)

Almshouse and workhouse

The purpose of the spread

This spread is designed to show what happened to the poor in Tudor times.

Background

The division between rich and poor has been a theme throughout this book and it is most apparent in the way in which provision was made for the poor.

As we now live in a society where there is considerable social provision, it will need a lot of imagination for students to consider a world in which there was almost none. It would also, as a matter of cross curricula work, be worth examining the nature of society in developing countries, where there is also little social provision even today. This would also allow students to understand what a big gulf there is between rich and poor globally today.

Students can think about one of the benefits of the Roman Catholic church as it was set up before Henry VIII as being a place where the poor could go for food. Because the church had lots of land and got rents from its farmers, the people were, in effect, paying for the poor without directly realising it.

After the reformation, the duty of looking after the poor fell on the parish and so was, in effect, a local tax. People then became much more aware of it. At the same time, the changes in land tenure meant that there were more people without a job.

Many towns still have almshouses, often dating back to Tudor times. These, and hospitals, were the result of bequests by local wealthy. But there was no co-ordinated system across the country.

Students will have to learn a different use of the word hospital as described in Tudor times.

The situation was chronic enough by later Tudor times for there to be a Poor Law (one of many) which aimed to raise money to pay for a national scheme of relief. But a distinction was made between the able bodied and the very young and old. It might be worth going over what age people could be regarded as able bodied. It might mean five years of age.

The able bodied were gathered into workhouses, a feature of society that prevailed for the better part of 400 years.

When George Whittaker died

Henry Parker was riding by the church with his friend Hugh Foulds.

"Who are they burying today?" asked Henry as he nodded towards a small group of people huddled round an open grave.

"It's George Whittaker," replied Hugh. "Didn't he used to work for you?"

"Yes. It's a long time ago now," confirmed Henry. "When we gave up growing corn and just farmed sheep, we had no work for him so he left."

"Well, things did not go well for him," said Hugh. "He lived in a hovel in Yarrow Wood and took what work he could find. He was a proud man and would not beg. Some say he starved to death."

Henry and Hugh rode to the crossroads, then parted. Henry was sad about George and decided to go and find where he had lived.

He dismounted at the edge of Yarrow Wood and followed a path through the bracken. In a short while he found a shelter made from branches, twigs and mud. Inside he found a scythe, rake, spade, axe, pitch fork, a cooking pot, a knife, a spoon and a blanket.

"This is all old George had in the world," thought Henry and compared it with his own large house and farm.

As Henry rode home he decided to give some of his money to the parish so six almshouses could be built for poor people like George. When Henry died he left even more money to the parish in his will to build a hospital.

1. Do you think George found much work after leaving Henry's farm? Explain your answer.

   ✎ ....

2. What is a hovel?

   ✎ ....

3. George's belongings could be divided into three groups according to three activities. What were the activities and what were the items in each group?

   ✎ ....

4. How do you think George's death helped other people in the parish?

   ✎ ....

When George Whittaker died

Age range
- Years 3/4 (SP4/5).
- Years 5/6 (SP6/7).

Resources
A copy of the worksheet.

Using the worksheet
We know about the wealth of rich people because they left wills but many poor people did not because they had so little to pass on to others. Tudors believed that people should look after themselves and many had little time for able bodied people who were poor. However, many people could not find enough work and some were too proud to beg. Rich people gave money in their wills to the poor but sometimes an incident made a rich person help the poor in their own lifetime.

Younger students
The students can read through the sheet and answer the questions. They may also draw a picture or series of pictures depicting scenes from the story.

Answers.
1. No. He did not have enough money to rent a home or possibly to buy food.
2. A shelter made out of branches, twigs and mud.
3. Work (scythe, rake, spade, axe, pitchfork) eating (cooking pot, knife, spoon), sleep (blanket).
4. The almshouses provided other poor people with a home. The hospital helped poor people who were ill.

Outcomes
The students:
- Know that some Tudors lived in great poverty.
- Know that some rich Tudors helped poor people.

Older students
The students can work through the sheet on their own. The answers are in the section above. You may like to explore with the students why Henry helped the poor by considering questions such as: Did Henry feel responsible for George's life and death? Did he just feel sorry for George and wished he could have done more? Did he feel that it was his duty to help the poor?

Outcomes
The students:
- Know that some Tudors lived in great poverty.
- Know that some rich Tudors helped poor people.
- Can explore reasons for helping the poor.

Spread ⑱ (pages 38–39)

Plague

THE TIMES OF QUEEN ELIZABETH AND AFTER

Plague

Rich and poor alike were likely to be struck down by disease. The only difference was whether you died in a comfortable bed or a hard one.

Tudor people had hard, often short lives. They usually had poor diets and lived in homes that were not kept clean.

This meant that diseases spread quickly. The most deadly disease was called PLAGUE. This had killed millions of people.

▼ ① Buildings were cramped and crowded, and no one cleared the rubbish from the streets. In these conditions it was easy for the plague to spread.

THE TIMES OF QUEEN ELIZABETH AND AFTER

Plague is an infection caused by tiny organisms called BACTERIA. People usually get plague from being bitten by fleas carrying the plague bacteria. The fleas live in the fur of rats and mice.

In Tudor times, once a person was infected, there were no useful medicines to cure the plague, so both rich and poor died equally.

In the worst outbreaks of plagues, such as in Norwich in 1579, as much as 30 or 40 per cent of the population died.

The trouble with towns

Towns suffered from disease more than the countryside because they were more crowded and filthier. In crowded, unclean conditions it is easier for infection to spread.

How had this come about? It was all caused by the rapid growth of the town in Tudor times (see pages 28–29 and picture ①).

To cope with the demand for places to live, landlords built ramshackle houses of very poor quality. Whole families lived in one room, and several families shared a small two-storey tenement.

Everyone threw their waste into the gutters that ran down the centres of the roads. The waste materials attracted rats. As a result, both streets and homes were alive with rats.

When a plague broke out, all that could be done was to make sure the people and their families were shut in their homes. A white cross was painted on to their doors.

People were confined in their homes for five weeks. Watchmen gave them food, but made sure they did not get out. They either died or, if they were lucky, got better.

38   39

The purpose of the spread

One of the great features of Tudor times, as in many other times before and after, was the spread of communicable diseases. This is a cross-curricular opportunity to study its causes and effect.

Background

This study can be made with an overlap to both Science (through 'Microbes') and Geography (through 'Water'). 'Microbes' is supported by our *Science@School* book *6B Microbes* and 'Water' is supported by our *Curriculum Visions* title *The Water Book.*

We have already alluded to the way in which hygiene was not a priority in Tudor England. This was, in part, because the benefits of hygiene were not understood, and because hygiene requires expensive solutions which people could not afford.

When you have no toilets, you have to fetch your water, you cannot heat up large amounts of water and you cannot afford soap, then the chances of good hygiene are slim.

Students might like to consider how to remain hygienic when you have no toilet paper and cannot get any newspaper (because there aren't newspapers). You can make a comparison back to 'Romans in Britain' and how they used sponges and water. By Tudor times the Roman standard had not been regained.

An infectious disease is an illness that you get through the effects of bacteria or viruses. Not all diseases can be transmitted between people. Cholera is an example. You only get it when you drink contaminated water. Some diseases are communicable and are called contagious. Those involving sneezing might be of this kind.

Plague is an infectious fever caused by a bacterium. It is carried by the rat flea. The fever affects all rodents and spreads infection between them. Many die, but we are not aware of that because rodents are nocturnal and not often seen on the surface.

When humans get the plague it is because they come into contact with the fleas of infected rodents.

There are three different kinds of plague affecting people: bubonic (where the lymph nodes swell), pneumonic (which affects the lungs) and septicemic (which gets into the bloodstream).

People do not normally get plague unless they accidentally get into the cycle by sharing the environment of the rodents and so getting bitten by the fleas. This allows the bacteria to get into the body.

When rat numbers are high and where rats can get into the living quarters of people, then there is a high chance that fleas can be transmitted to people.

Plague shows itself when the number of bacteria in the body reach a critical level. As a result there is a delay between infection and the onset of the illness. And when it begins it is usually sudden.

Bubonic plague starts with shivering, then being sick, violent headaches, giddiness, wish to stay out of the light, and general pain in the back and limbs. Fever is common. Lumps appear in the armpits and groin.

Bubonic plague is not contagious, but if the sufferer gets affected in the lungs and develops pneumonic plague then they will become contagious and give pneumonic plague to others.

Make a plague mask

1. Take a piece of A4 card and bend it into a cone. Cut off some of the edges at the open end to make a rim about 8 cm in diameter (see figure 1). Use sticky paper to hold the card in a cone shape.

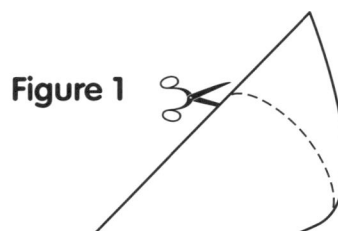

2. Take a large thin elastic band and stick it to one part of the rim with sticky tape as figure 2 shows.

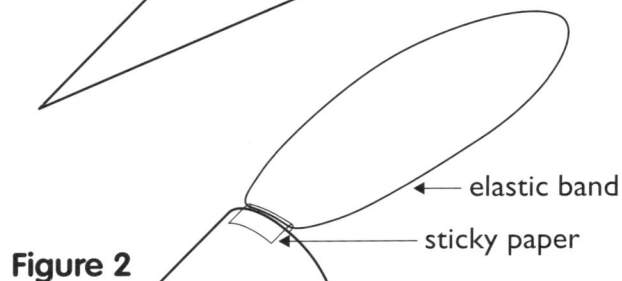

3. Take a piece of cloth about one metre long and by 70 cm wide and lay it on a table. Place the cone upright at about 30 cm from one end. Draw round the cone. Mark two places for eye holes (figure 3).

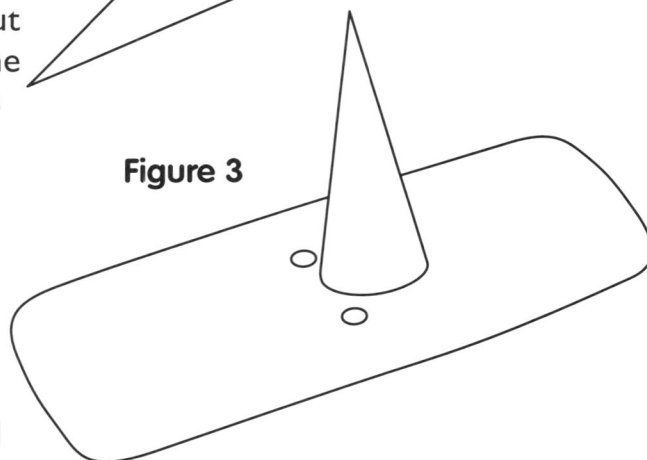

4. Cut a hole inside the circle you have drawn. Cut small holes for the eye holes.

5. Put the cone over your nose and hold it in place with the elastic band positioned between your eyebrows and the top of the back of your head.

6. Carefully pull the cloth over the cone and move the cloth around so that you can see through the eye holes.

7. Wear a hat such as a duck hat to get the effect of a Tudor doctor visiting a patient with the plague (figure 4).

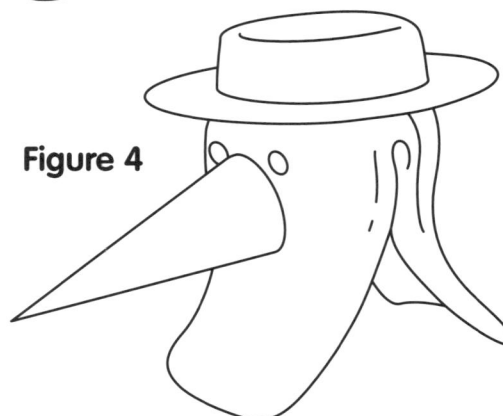

Figure 1

Figure 2

elastic band
sticky paper

Figure 3

Figure 4

116

Make a plague mask

Age range

- Years 3/4 (SP4/5).
- Years 5/6 (SP6/7).

Resources

Each person making a mask will need an A4 sheet of thin card, a long thin elastic band, sticky paper, scissors, a sheet of cloth about one metre long by 70 cm wide. The cloth should be one colour preferably grey or white. A duck hat or similar "pie shaped" hat. Older students need secondary sources about plague masks.

Using the worksheet

Like everyone else, doctors were terrified of the plague. A symptom of the plague was the production of large boils. Doctors were called to deal with the boils in the following way. They had to put the end of a metal rod in a fire then touch the end onto the boil. This would make the boil explode. To prevent them getting the plague, doctors wore a plague mask. Although it looked like a beak it was in fact a holder of herbs which had a sweet smell. It was thought that this would give the doctor some protection from the plague. The plague masks were scary and must have done little to comfort the patient. The students could make their masks at school or at home. They could give the eye holes more support by making cardboard discs and cutting holes in the centre then sticking the discs over the holes in the cloth.

Younger students

The students may like to work in pairs as they will need to help each other when they are sticking the cardboard to make the cone and when putting on the cloth over the cone. Students who wear spectacles should remove them before they put on the cone. Be prepared for a reaction from the class when the first person wears a plague mask.

Outcomes

The students can:
- Follow instructions and work together.
- Use materials safely.
- Appreciate how the plague mask scared people.

Older students

The students may assemble their own masks but will need help in making the cones and putting on the cloth and cone. They can look at secondary sources about plague masks and compare them with the masks they have made.

Outcomes

The students can:
- Use materials safely to assemble a plague mask.
- Assess the accuracy of the model they have made using secondary sources.

Spread ⑲ (pages 40–41)

Learning

The purpose of the spread

To make a contrast between the way people learned in Tudor times and that of today by describing some of the features of Tudor education.

Background

We are not all gifted in the same direction. Some of us are academically gifted, some socially gifted, some gifted with their hands and so on.

Today, schools try to foster each of these achievements, within the framework of a curriculum.

Do children know why they are at school? Have they ever talked it out and thought through the idea of compulsory education?

People in Tudor times did not get compulsory education. They had to pay for it. But in many ways they were much luckier than the students who went before them because, during Tudor times, education became to be seen as an important way of getting on in life.

Different parts of society had differing reasons for wanting to get on. Those who were wealthy didn't have to think about a job, so their efforts went into social skills, and for this the fad was to learn Latin. Latin would also act as a passport to the church.

Yeomen farmers and others who were not wealthy, but could afford to pay a little, knew what they wanted out of education. They wanted to get their children the basic educational skills that might get them into the church or into a profession. If they could do this they could become wealthy and support their parents when they became old. It was not clear whether what you learned was of direct use. But if you had learned what was on offer, you could advance up the professional ladder.

In fact, what was on offer was Mathematics, Latin and Greek. Part of the reason for this was that many teachers came from the church, especially when monks were looking for a job after the dissolution of the monasteries. It might not have been of any direct use, and indeed, the learning process was not at that time designed to produce a spirit of enquiry. But all children did know why they were there, and if they forgot, there was always the whipping post to remind them.

For those who wanted a trade – and this, too, was an avenue to success – apprenticeships were the way forward. Students should notice that, as in all other forms of education, parents had to pay for apprenticeships.

Make a horn book

1. Mark out the dimensions shown in figure 1 on a piece of corrugated cardboard then cut out the shape. The cardboard represents a piece of wood.

2. Cut out a rectangle of transparent plastic a little smaller than the main part of the cardboard as shown in figure 2. The plastic represents a layer of transparent horn.

3. Write an alphabet using the letters in activity **6D** on a piece of paper that is a little smaller than the piece of plastic.

4. Assemble the cardboard paper and plastic as shown in figure 2 and make holes through the plastic and card or ask your teacher to make them.

5. Push a split pin through each hole and splay the ends underneath to hold the items in place.

6. Use the hornbooks to refer to the Tudor alphabet when writing letters and documents.

Figure 1

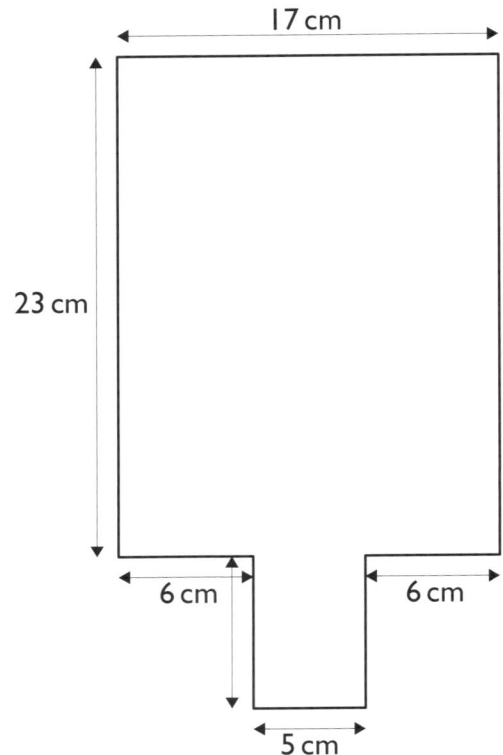

17 cm

23 cm

6 cm   6 cm

5 cm

Figure 2

held together with split pins

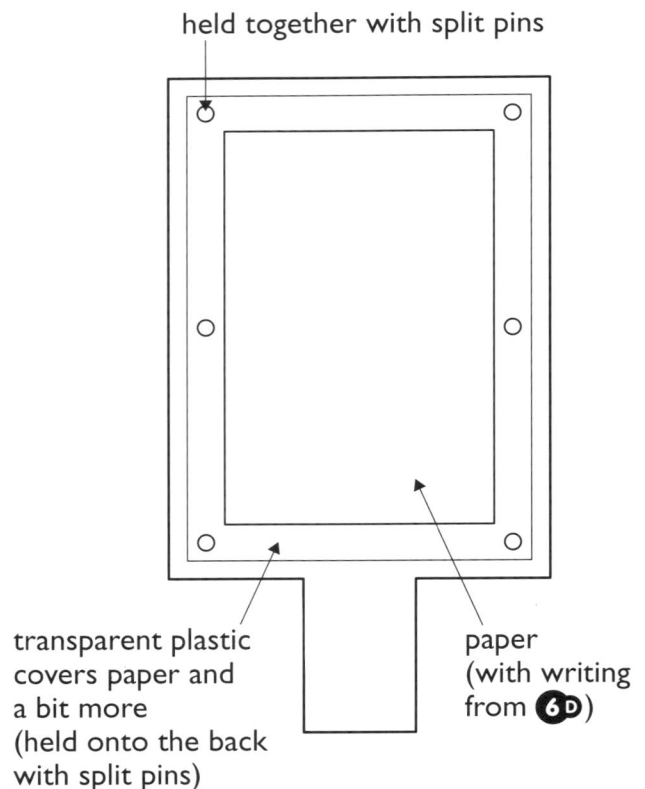

transparent plastic covers paper and a bit more (held onto the back with split pins)

paper (with writing from **6D**)

Make a horn book

Age range
- Years 3/4 (SP4/5).
- Years 5/6 (SP6/7).

Resources
A piece of cardboard, a piece of transparent plastic, a piece of paper, access to the worksheet in activity **6D**, pencil, ruler, scissors, split pins.

Using the worksheet
School children used a hornbook as a reference for the alphabet. They hung the hornbook from a belt. If you are having a Tudor day you might like the students to make the hornbook beforehand so that they can use it to write a Tudor letter. They may attach the hornbook to their belts with a piece of string.

Younger students
The students can work through the sheet but you may feel that you should make the holes for them.

Outcomes
The students can:
- Construct a model hornbook.

Older students
The students can work through the sheet. You may feel that some students can make the holes for themselves.

Outcomes
The students can:
- Construct a model hornbook.

Black lettering

Black lettering is a style of writing that was used for many kinds of important documents in Tudor times.

a b c d e f g h i

j l k m n o p q r s t

u v w x y z A B C

D E F G H I J

K L M N O P Q

R S T U V W

X Y Z

Black lettering

Age range
- Years 3/4 (SP4/5).
- Years 5/6 (SP6/7).

Resources
Copies of the worksheet, tracing paper, paste, paper, pencil or pen. For more advanced work a broad nibbed pen is needed and a calligraphy book showing how to construct some of the letters.

Using the worksheet
The writing of black lettering needs the support of a calligraphy book but the students can learn how to recognise black lettering in important documents by trying the tracing activity here.

Younger students
The students can trace the letters to make their first name and then cut them out and stick them on a sheet of paper neatly. They may also like to write their full name and their address.

Outcomes
The students can:
- Recognise black lettering.
- Assemble letters written in the black lettering style neatly.

Older students
The students may try the tracing activity described for younger students or they may try and copy some of the letters onto a line ruled on a piece of paper. Interested students could extend the work by using a calligraphy pen and book to construct a simple notice or document.

Outcomes
The students can:
- Recognise black lettering.
- Assemble letters written in the black lettering style neatly.
- Write in the black lettering style by copying the letters.

Make a pen

Tudor boys had pen knives. They used them at school to turn large feathers into pens. The waxy tip of the feather was cut at an angle and the tip then had a slit cut in it. When the tip was dipped in ink it held some around the slit. When the tip was pressed onto paper ink flowed down the slit. If the pen tip was moved a line of ink was made on the paper. A pen made from a feather is called a quill.

Can a plastic straw be used as a pen?

1. Use scissors to cut the end of a plastic straw (figure 1a) at an angle (figure 1b).

Figure 1a

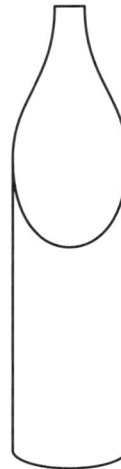

Figure 1b

2. Cut a slit in the end of the straw as figure 2 shows.

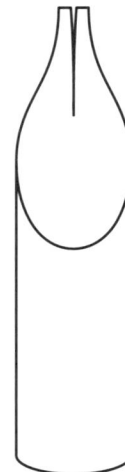

Figure 2

3. Dip the end of the straw in ink, then try and write a letter on paper. Dip again to write more letters.

4. Modern ink pens are called fountain pens. They contain ink which is released through a metal nib. Try writing with a fountain pen. How does it compare with writing with your straw pen.

Make a pen

Age range
- Years 3/4 (SP4/5).
- Years 5/6 (SP6/7).

Resources
Each student will need a plastic drinking straw, a pair of scissors, ink, white paper, access to a fountain pen.

Using the worksheet
The students may be surprised to find that a pen knife was actually used to turn a feather into a pen. The pen was called a quill pen. School boys had to make their own quill pens at school before they could start to write. If you can obtain some large feathers such as goose feathers, and none of the students are allergic to feathers, you could demonstrate how to make a quill pen.

Younger students
Cutting the end of the stalk and making the slit are quite tricky and most students may need help. You may prefer to cut the ends of the straws for the students and just let them try to write with them. They can use a fountain pen without assistance.

Outcomes
The students can:
- Appreciate the difficulties in making and using a pen.
- Write neatly with a fountain pen.

Older students
The students may be able to make their own straw pens. They could experiment with fine and blunt tips. If none are allergic to feathers they could try and make a quill pen. Make sure the activity follows your school policy for health and safety.

Outcomes
The students can:
- Appreciate the difficulties in making and using a pen.
- Write neatly with a fountain pen.

Spread ㉒ (pages 42–43)

Exploration

The purpose of the spread

To show how exploration was a complex affair having many purposes.

Background

This spread on exploration allows students to research one of the most remarkable of Tudor sailors – Sir Francis Drake.

From a previous spread they will understand the nature of apprenticeship. But they will also appreciate how lucky Drake was to be left a ship in a will. Without it, the capital for all subsequent adventures might have been lacking.

Drake is an example of someone of humble beginnings who became very wealthy as a result of a combination of skill, cunning, success at politics and a buccaneering spirit. He makes an interesting comparison with entrepreneurs today. It will, perhaps, show that principles haven't changed much.

Using this spread it is also possible to discuss – as a cross-curricula activity with Geography – just how little was known of the New World. Cabot, for example, who sailed at the start of Tudor times, believed himself to be in a location that was half a world away from where he really intended. It shows how important the construction of accurate maps is, and how little information explorers had to work with. It also showed the political advantage of setting a foot on a land which you can later claim to be your own.

The bargain between Elizabeth I and Drake was an interesting one, where Drake was given permission to work for the crown, but it was left up to him to finance it. And if financing was done at the misfortune of an enemy power in Europe, then this was a political advantage for Elizabeth.

Exploration at this time was not the same as settlement, although one followed the other after a substantial interval.

Journeys of exploration

Use a world map in an atlas to help you plot the following journey.

Sir Francis Drake's journey round the world

Drake sailed down the English Channel and down the coast of Spain and Africa. After he passed the Cape Verde Islands, he crossed the Atlantic Ocean and sailed down the coast of South America. He sailed round Cape Horn and up the west coast of South America and North America to just south of San Diego. From here he sailed across the Pacific Ocean to Borneo then through the gap between Sumatra and Java to the Cape of Good Hope. He sailed north to the coast near Liberia then back up to the English Channel, and home.

Journeys of exploration

Age range
- Years 3/4 (SP4/5).
- Years 5/6 (SP6/7).

Resources
A photocopy of the sheet. You may wish to use the larger map on page 134 of this book. An atlas with a map of the world.

Using the worksheet
You may like to use the worksheet after the students have read about Drake on pages 42 and 43 of the student book. There is a full A4 size map on page 134 of this book which can also be used for this activity.

Younger students
The students may need help locating some of the places on the world map and identifying the features on the map on the worksheet. If some students finish early, they could try some of the questions in the section for older students.

Outcomes
The students can:
- Identify locations on a map.
- Chart the journey of a ship around the world.

Older students
The students can work on their own and you may wish to extend the exercise by writing these questions on the board and asking the students to plot the journeys. The students could then use secondary sources to find out more about the explorers.
1. Sir Martin Frobisher sailed from the English Channel to the southern coast of Greenland and then to near the southern tip of Baffin Island.
2. John Cabot sailed from the English Channel to Newfoundland.

3. Sir Walter Raleigh sailed from the English Channel to the North American coast about a quarter of the way from Washington to Miami. The students could look at more detailed maps of the east coast of the United States to find Roanoke island.
4. Richard Chancellor sailed through the North Sea and around Norway to Archangel.

Outcomes
The students can:
- Identify locations on a map.
- Plot the journeys of ships across the world.

Spread ㉑ (pages 44–45)

Settlers

The purpose of the spread

This spread completes the book and more or less completes the Tudor Age. The events began at the very end of Elizabeth I's reign and, of course, moved forward with great vigour under the Stewarts.

Background

There is no longer any land to settle in the way that was true at the end of the 17th century. So it is very difficult to imagine what people must have felt about it.

It may be worthwhile going over the dimensions of the ships used to cross the Atlantic. How much could they carry as provisions? How would they be able to cope with the weather? What backup was there if things went wrong?

In general going to settle in the Americas was as risky as a modern settlement on the Moon. It was a stupendous act of faith. In the case of the early settlers it failed. Of course, later on it had unbounded success.

So it is worth looking at the problems that might have been confronted and why things went wrong. For example, they sailed to a land which had a different climate. Where they landed was a coastal swamp. It would have been heavily infested with mosquitoes. It was heavily forested. There was no chance of getting a crop within the first few months and they had not been able to carry a reserve with them, so the whole adventure was pretty precarious from the start.

Many of the people were extremely naive about the journey and its hardships. However, it is clear they set up cabins after the fashion of those built in Tudor villages. They had already imported a European style.

They were forced to find food by dealing with the people who already lived in the area. But they were not skilled at dealing with other peoples as equals. As a result there were arguments and the supply of food was cut off.

When settlers move in

Imagine you were a North American Indian living on an island with your family and friends. You have more than enough food and materials for all your needs. Another group of people arrive on the island. They are English settlers. They do not speak your language but possess many useful items that you do not have. They appear to be friendly.

1. At first you make them welcome. Why did you do this?

   ✎ ....

2. You see that they are having difficulty surviving on the island. What help could you offer?

   ✎ ....

3. The settlers still struggle to survive and ask for more and more help. How do their actions affect:

   (i) the survival of your own group?

   ✎ ....

   (ii) your relationship with them?

   ✎ ....

4. Imagine you are a settler.

   (i) How do you think your settling on the island could help the local people?

   ✎ ....

   (ii) How did you feel asking for help?

   ✎ ....

   (iii) As you are having difficulty surviving on the island how do you think the problem could be solved?

   ✎ ....

When settlers move in

Age range
- Years 3/4 (SP4/5).
- Years 5/6 (SP6/7).

Resources
A photocopy of the sheet.

Using the worksheet
You can use the worksheet to let the children explore how people feel when new people come to their lands and how settlers feel in a new country.

Younger students
Let the students work through the questions – here are some answers but there could be others:

1. There is enough food and materials to share. The people have items that they may be willing to trade. The people may have useful skills that can help both groups survive.
2. Help them grow their own food and make homes to withstand the weather.
3. (i) Our group may use food and materials it needs to help the settlers and this will affect our own survival. If we spend too much time helping them, we will not have enough time to help ourselves.
    (ii) There would be anger and resentment on our part because the settlers cannot help themselves and ask for too much.
4. (i) We could bring items to trade and new skills to help them.
    (ii) At first you might feel a little ashamed. Later you would dread asking for help and feel foolish because you cannot acquire the skills to survive.
    (iii) By moving to the mainland. By going back to England.

Outcomes
The students can:
- Appreciate the difficulties of people who have settlers on their lands.
- Appreciate the difficulties of settlers in a new land.

Older students
The students could work in groups. Some could address questions 1 to 3, other groups could address question 4 and think up more questions to explore about settling in a foreign land. The groups could then present their findings followed by a whole class discussion.

Outcomes
The students can:
- Appreciate the difficulties of people who have settlers on their lands.
- Appreciate the difficulties of settlers in a new land.

Journeys of exploration

Name:...

Form:.............................

Notes

Notes